Praise for *Elite Minds*

I hired Doctor Stan Beecham as team sport psychologist while he was a young doctoral student at the University of Georgia, and he was a tremendous help with our football team, especially working with the kickers through our kicking coach. One of the beneficiaries of that decision was our field goal kicker, All-American Kevin Butler, who today is the only such kicker to be inducted in the College Football Hall of Fame. I was proud to have read Stan's book *Elite Minds* and highly recommend it for athletes, sports enthusiasts, and the general public.

—Vince Dooley, College Football Hall of Fame inductee,
UGA football coach, UGA athletics director

In a virtual sea of business improvement books, *Elite Minds* will stand out as one of the greats. Dr. Stan's message that "expectation dictates performance" is critical. All leaders "want to win," yet few "expect to win." At Vonage, we've internalized this view, and *Elite Minds* is required reading for our managers and leaders. I wholeheartedly recommend *Elite Minds* to anyone who wants to create a winning mindset within their organization.

—Alan Masarek, CEO, Vonage

I can't put this new book down! I've long been a fan of sport psychologist Dr. Stan Beecham. In fact, I hired him as the psychologist for my elite running team a few years ago. Now he has published his long-awaited book on peak performance called *Elite Minds* . . . I'm really glad he wrote this book. It truly is a great read and I'm very excited to offer it to the McMillan community. *Buy it. Read it. Get ready for the performances of your dreams.*

—Greg McMillan, founder, McMillan Running

I enjoyed *Elite Minds* and purchased copies for family and coworkers. Stan presents invaluable information and ideas for success in your personal life and the highly competitive business environment.

—Mike Cote, CEO, SecureWorks

I find *Elite Minds* by Dr. Beecham to be a great resource for me and my athletes. We use it as a training manual for the mental aspects of the game and it has paid great dividends. I highly recommend it whether you are a coach or a team looking for better skills.

—Manny Diaz, University of Georgia men's tennis coach
and six-time NCAA Team Championship winner

Dr. Stan has worked with our leaders for many years, challenging us not only in our pursuits to be a high-performing team but also to understand ourselves and what might be keeping us from realizing our professional and personal ambitions. This includes setting ambitious goals and accepting failure versus staying in our comfort zones. *Elite Minds* captures in a very effective manner the tough questions and directness that is classic Dr. Stan.

—Jim Burke, CEO, TXU Energy

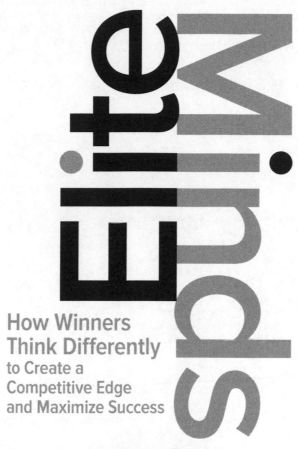

Elite Minds

How Winners Think Differently
to Create a
Competitive Edge
and Maximize Success

Dr. Stan Beecham

Mc
Graw
Hill
Education

New York   Chicago   San Francisco   Athens   London
Madrid   Mexico City   Milan   New Delhi
Singapore   Sydney   Toronto

3 4 5 6 7 8 9 10   LCR   21 20 19 18 17

ISBN: 978-1-259-83616-9
MHID: 1-259-83616-9

e-ISBN: 978-1-259-83617-6
e-MHID: 1-259-83617-7

Library of Congress Cataloging-in-Publication Data
Names: Beecham, Stan, author.
Title: Elite minds: how winners think differently to create a competitive
   edge and maximize success / Dr. Stan Beecham.
Description: 1 Edition. | New York : McGraw-Hill Education, 2016.
Identifiers: LCCN 2016021236 (print) | LCCN 2016030663 (ebook) | ISBN
   9781259836169 (hardback : alk. paper) | ISBN 1259836169 (alk. paper) |
   ISBN 9781259836176 () | ISBN 1259836177 ()
Subjects: LCSH: Success. | Self-confidence. | Competition (Psychology) |
   BISAC: BUSINESS & ECONOMICS / Skills.
Classification: LCC BF637.S8 B387 2016 (print) | LCC BF637.S8 (ebook) | DDC
   158.1--dc23
LC record available at https://lccn.loc.gov/2016021236

McGraw-Hill Education books are available at special quantity discounts to use as premiums and sales promotions or for use in corporate training programs. To contact a representative, please visit the Contact Us pages at www.mhprofessional.com.

This book is dedicated to all who wish to fly.

DISCLAIMER

Do not read this book if you are looking for a quick fix, motivation, or just want to feel better. There is no such thing. Happy is for children. Being happy is not the purpose of your life. Being fully alive and awake is the purpose of your life. That includes the pain and struggle that is a critical and necessary component to human existence.

There are no 7 Habits, 15 Characteristics, or 21 Laws. There are no Secrets or Promises. If you desire a book that shows you the precise steps to a successful outcome, may I recommend a good cookbook—Julia Child's, to be specific. However, I can promise you that your casserole will not turn out like hers, even if you do exactly what she suggests, in the exact order she recommends. Life is the same way. We think that by following someone else's recipe we will reach our destination. No, you will reach their destination, which will, in turn, mean you are still lost.

If you haven't bought the book yet, put it down and go back to the magazines; they will make you happy and distract you from waking the hell up and getting on with it (especially the ones with lots of pictures). That will make your friends, family, competitors, and enemies very happy.

If you are still reading, good—there is hope for you. However, reading this book will likely make you feel worse, not better. But hey, you were not born to be content, you were born to be complete (that's what the word "perfect" means), to be the greatest "you" possible—and the fact of the matter is, very few make it. That journey involves giving up the hope that someone else is going to give you the answer or set a plan for you that will fulfill your life-long dreams. Anyone who has the audacity to suggest that others follow their path because in the eyes of the world they have been deemed successful is simply practicing narcissism. What I have attempted to do with this book is share with you my observations of people who have successfully navigated from Point A to Point B in as straight a line as possible for a human to maneuver. They have performed at the highest of levels possible—not because they followed someone else's advice, but because they had the courage to take their own.

Contents

Foreword

In August 1996, I walked onto the University of Georgia campus ready to play collegiate golf for one of the most decorated women's golf programs in the country. I was internally motivated by my goals of gaining an education while hoping to equip myself with the tools to take my game to an even higher level. As a student-athlete, I wanted to use all of my resources to help me achieve my goals of one day playing on the Ladies Professional Golf Tour (LPGA). I had always lived by the quote, "Champions are made, not born!" I was motivated to be great!

Beans Kelly, my head coach at the University of Georgia, called a team meeting one August afternoon at the beginning of our fall season. It was a group session to start some work with our athletic department's sport psychologist. I will never forget that moment when Dr. Stan Beecham entered the room to start his lesson on team cohesion and personal beliefs. I was intrigued by what he said that day. Dr. Beecham lit a fire in me to become curious about my golf game and myself. He made me ask myself the question, "What is missing inside of me that might be holding me back?" I wanted to explore this question even further, but was frightened by what I might find out about myself. Dr. Beecham could sense that my wheels were turning and I was hungry to learn more. From that first encounter in fall semester, my life was forever changed. I knew I was good at the game of golf, but he helped me cultivate a plan to become great!

Dr. Beecham asked me the tough questions and forced me to face my biggest fears. By facing those fears, I was able to free up my mind to play golf in a way that I had never dreamed would be possible. We had weekly meetings and worked consistently on creating a system of beliefs about myself that led to some amazing results both on and off the golf course.

Creating a consistent discipline to train my mind daily to believe that I belonged at the top allowed me to perform at the highest level week in and week out. I became a four-time All-American, Southeastern Conference Freshman of the Year, two-time Southeastern Conference Player of the Year, and numerous individual and team titles were added to my resume. Dr. Beecham convinced me to believe that winning was a habit and that mental focus and practice was more important than my technical training.

I always knew that college was a stepping-stone for my future life and would give me the tools to face the real world after graduation. Dr. Beecham helped me transform my inner self to a place that I am proud to stand today.

Due to an early diagnosis of rheumatoid arthritis, my professional golf career was cut short. Fortunately, I was able to stay in the game of golf as the head women's golf coach at the University of Arkansas. Dr. Beecham has remained a huge resource even to this day as I work tirelessly to provide a mental toughness and competitive environment that allows my teams to compete at the highest level. He continues to make me hungry to reach outside of my boundaries and to think consistently outside of the box. As humans, we are often uncomfortable being different or not doing the norm, but the thing I love most about my time with Dr. Beecham is his constant prodding and a persistence to try the impossible.

I admire Dr. Beecham for finally reaching out and doing what he thought was impossible by writing this book. *Elite Minds* is a window into his spirit and into his unique perspective on how to outthink the competition. I have been blessed to learn about this for over fifteen years now. It will challenge you to take a risk and to look at things differently. It is a great lesson on gratitude and setting an intention for a journey. I hope his words inspire you as much as they have forever changed me as a person and a coach.

Shauna Estes-Taylor
University of Arkansas Head Women's Golf Coach
Inductee: NGCA Players Hall of Fame

Introduction

Everyone needs a coach. Coaching and leadership matter. They just do. Great coaches teach us the hardest and most helpful lessons about life. Think back over the course of your life to the coaches who really mattered. The really good ones took interest in you and time to get to know you without your even realizing it. They figured out what made you tick. They pushed you. They lectured you. They argued with you. They raised their voices at you. They helped you win and never made it about them. They picked you up after you lost, made a mistake, or used bad judgment and got you back on your feet. They didn't do it for the money, and they didn't count their hours in helping you. We have all asked ourselves why they did it, and we have thought how lucky we were to be in their presence. Maybe they saw some of themselves in us. Maybe they could see our unfulfilled potential, or they saw us as just needing a chance or a break. In the end, it didn't matter why. What did matter was that good coaching helped us become our best.

Shortly after taking on a new leadership role in January 2009, I began to think about how and why certain people perform at a higher level than others, even with the same tools and resources. I began to research and study the concept of what creates exceptional performance. Great coaching is a core element of high performance—nobody has achieved it without the help of others. My belief was that if I could study the concept of high performance, I could actually perform at a higher level and lead those around me to an even greater level of performance. So I read and studied a number of books and attended many programs and lectures on the topic of performance, but something just wasn't clicking. Then, I discovered Stan Beecham and his book *Elite Minds*. I read the first few pages, and I knew I had found something special.

The book had really caught my attention. I decided to contact Stan because I was fascinated with a number of the topics in the book. I wanted to discuss them in greater detail in terms of how they affected me and those I lead. Each day, I was able to see how the concepts in the book were relative to me both personally and professionally. Stan took my call, and we have been working together ever since. He has helped me raise my performance across many dimensions of my life. I also introduced him to the teams and individuals who work with me, and I have witnessed how his work has increased their performance and made their lives fuller as well.

As I reflect on Stan's work with me, three things immediately come to my mind. First, he has challenged my thinking with the idea of not trying to be better but instead, being my best. Second, Stan's book helped me understand the theory of why people perform differently. Third, and most importantly, I learned that those who perform at the highest level possible do not follow someone else's advice but, instead, have the courage to take their own advice.

Simply stated, Stan is a great coach. As you read this book, you will experience it through his words but it is even more powerful to spend time with Stan. I have been blessed with several great coaches over the course of my life. Stan came to me at the perfect time in my professional career as a business leader and in my personal life as a husband and father. After reading Stan's book and working with him, members of my team have approached me and said that my ability to provide a coach to help them get to a higher level of performance has been a distinguishing quality of my leadership. *Elite Minds* has helped me be my best, and this book will help you to be your best.

Gregory M. McGauley
Financial Services Executive
Boston, Massachusetts

PART I

Understanding
Your Mind

1

Mind Over Matter

*If you plan on being anything less than you
are capable of being, you will probably
be unhappy all the days of your life.*

—ABRAHAM MASLOW

The debate continues, whether it's in business or competitive sport: How much of one's performance is based on physical ability, and how much of one's performance is based on mental acuity? Perhaps Yogi Berra said it best when he explained, "Baseball is 90 percent mental, and the other half is physical." From where I sit, the view's a little different. I believe the degree to which one performs and the level of success one achieves is 100 percent mental.

Why?

Because the mind is in control of the body.

This is not my opinion—it is scientifically verified by those who have studied the brain-mind complex for decades. Your brain is the software, your body the hardware. Simply put, your body does what your brain tells it to do or what your brain thinks your body is capable of doing.

Misunderstandings about the keys to performance exist because we have a bias toward the physical. In predicting success today, both coaches and business leaders are drunk on the elixir of talent and experience. We believe that if you can find a talented person who has matured with experience, then you should select that person for your team.

Sport is more swayed by talent, and business more so by experience, but they both look to those two attributes as the primary determinants of success. Unfortunately, it's not the best way to go about it. In fact, talent and experience alone will never lead to a sustained high level of performance—especially at the elite level in any given field.

The problem with this approach is that everyone is talented and has years of experience at the elite level. Who then performs the best when the advantages of talent and experience are mitigated?

The answer is simple: the person whose mind is an asset, not an obstruction.

The competitive advantage at the highest level is overwhelmingly mental, not physical.

I see this every day.

Mentality in Action

There are thousands of talented kids in college who never make it in the pros, and there are extremely bright and knowledgeable managers who fail to advance beyond the director or vice president level. These are the people I am frequently called in to work with. In a corporate setting, the conversation usually begins like this:

"Dr. Stan, we have this manager who is very bright and talented but is struggling to get her team performing at the level we need them to be. She has a great education and has worked at some of the best companies in our industry, but she is not having the impact we expected."

In a sports setting, coaches usually talk in terms of an athlete's not reaching his or her full potential:

"The kid's got raw talent. He even looks great in practice and at times makes it look effortless. But when I put him in the game, he's a totally different person."

A similar phenomenon is found in schools, where we observe smart kids who are unable to process information when taking a test. We call it "test anxiety" and shake our heads.

Before I further explain how such underachievement occurs, let's make some terms clear from the get-go so there is no confusion when we talk about the relationship between our minds and our performance.

To begin, what you need to know about your operating system— the brain—is that the way in which the brain functions is referred to as the mind. You can see a brain, but you can't see a mind.

Understanding the Mind

The mind is divided into two major categories: the conscious and the unconscious. The conscious mind is the part of your brain you are aware of. This is where you think, plan, solve problems, and experience emotions. The unconscious mind is a powerful determinant of behavior. It houses what you believe—that is, the things you hold as truth. Unfortunately, most people are unaware of their unconscious mind and the beliefs they hold to be true. Typically, while we are keenly aware of what we think and feel (conscious), the majority of us have very little understanding of what we really believe about ourselves and the world around us (unconscious). And this is where performance shortcomings arise. What you believe about yourself and your world is the primary determinant of what you do and, ultimately, how well you do it.

This is not a new idea. While Sigmund Freud still catches a lot of grief for his psychosexual hypotheses, he ultimately made a name for himself by bringing the unconscious mind to the forefront of psychology. To understand how this came about, you should know that Freud did not begin as a psychologist. Freud actually began as a neurologist, studying such diseases as cerebral palsy and other neuromuscular disorders.

Patients would come to Freud with tangible physical defects and limitations. Much to his own surprise, Freud was frequently unable to find any physical cause for the patients' paralysis, blindness, or pain. There was simply no physical explanation for the symptoms the patients exhibited.

Fortunately for us, Freud was a very curious and brilliant man who was unwilling to settle for a simple "I'm sorry your arm is paralyzed, but I can't help you" response. Instead, Freud stayed at it and began to talk to patients about the other things happening in their lives. This is where he struck gold.

Freud soon realized that the cause of many disorders was not physical but mental. Often, the patient's mind was the problem. The unconscious mind was causing the body to fail to perform properly. Back in Freud's day, this groundbreaking discovery was at first scorned by the entire medical community. Today, the mind-body relationship is widely accepted as ailments like stress and anxiety remain leading causes of health issues nationwide. Furthermore, they are the leading causes of sudden drops in performance—whether on the ball field or in the boardroom. Unfortunately, the medical and athletic communities aren't completely sold on the power of the mind. I'd be lying if I said I thought the medical and fitness communities are doing anything more than paying lip service to this most important of issues— the unconscious mind-body connection.

The truth is that we still prefer to initiate performance improvement and longevity from a tangible standpoint, and then we look at other alternative options if that doesn't work. While approaches like surgery, physical therapy, physical training regimens, and diets certainly hold their value and always will, we will continually fail to reach performance goals until we learn to utilize the engine of our minds.

The Role of Stress

Years ago, I attended a sport psychology conference where I noticed that a prominent orthopedic surgeon, Dr. Richard Steadman, would be speaking that day. Steadman had operated on many great athletes. (If you remember, Kobe Bryant was getting his knee worked on by Steadman when he made headlines in Colorado.) At first, I was curious as to why a surgeon would be speaking at a sport psychology conference, but, given the options during that hour, he seemed like the most interesting choice.

What Dr. Steadman said that day has never left my mind. Dr. Steadman acknowledged how modern medicine has thoroughly researched and documented the role stress and other mental maladies play in the onset of disease and illness. He was there that day not only to validate modern medicine's findings but also to take them a step further. He was there to share his belief that there is a relationship between one's mental state and accidental injury.

Steadman explained that when he would meet a new patient for the first time, he would ask a simple question: "What happened?" Over the years, he began to notice that people were less apt to give him physical reasons for the accident and more likely to offer him psychological explanations for how they became injured.

He didn't hear this type of explanation too often: "I was skiing along and hit a patch of ice that caused me to fall, and my leg bent backward. That's when I heard a pop." Instead, his patients' explanations were more often along these lines: "My wife and I were arguing because I wanted to hit the slopes and she wanted me to wait another 30 minutes for her to get ready. I told her I was going to make one quick run and then meet her at Lionshead in an hour. So I hurried up the mountain and flew down the hill to make sure I met her on time, and that's when I fell awkwardly and heard a pop."

Keep in mind that Dr. Steadman is not some peripheral quack who is talking to sport psychologists because he has lost the respect of his peers. He is one of the leading doctors in his field. You don't make an appointment with him; you request one. If you need knee surgery, there are only a handful of elite options, and he is one of them.

His message to us that day was that accidents don't just happen. There are psychological antecedents to all human behavior, even accidents. In other words, every physical event is preceded by a psychological event. Could it be true? I believe so, and in the pages that follow, I'll explain precisely why. For now, let me continue setting the stage with a few more thought-provoking examples from my own experience.

The Real Reasons Injuries Happen

One of the most interesting conversations I have ever had with a coach was with Tubby Smith, the former basketball coach at the University of Georgia, while we were both getting dressed in the men's locker room. I had noticed that his athletes were not getting injured at the same rate as athletes on other teams. I asked Tubby why he thought this was true.

His reply was simple and precise, "I tell my team we are not going to get injured. We will do the things we need to do to prevent injury, and we will warm up before practice and do some exercises to keep us strong, but we will simply not get injured."

Tubby clearly understood what very few other coaches do—that injury rate is closely correlated with a belief system. Tubby believed his team was not going to get injured, and they believed what he said. Compare this to the belief system that most coaches have. How many times have you heard a coach say, "Injury is unfortunately just a part of the game. You enter every season knowing that some athletes will get hurt. It's unavoidable. You just hope the injury bug doesn't bite your key guys at important times."

Some teams have recurring problems with injuries that keep them from ever reaching their full potential. But if you were to suggest that a large part of the cause was psychological, most coaches would just laugh at you. Unfortunately, these same coaches would miss one of the most important keys to their success.

This same dynamic is true in business. Show me the number of sick days a company has per employee, and I can accurately predict the psychological health of the company culture. There is more to "accident prone" people than meets the eye.

THE HIGH COST OF STRESS

Illness and injury are huge factors in a business's financial success as well. Some estimates suggest that approximately 50 percent of corporate profits go toward healthcare. American companies lose between $200 and $300 billion each year in stress-related illness and lost productivity.

Unscheduled absences cost employers $3,600 per hourly employee per year and $2,650 per salaried employee per year. The American Medical Association has stated that stress is the cause of 80 to 85 percent of all illness and disease.

Recently, I read *The Biology of Belief* by Dr. Bruce Lipton. If you are interested in digging deeper into the relationship between mind and body, you will find his book intriguing. Lipton begins one chapter with a story about a Dr. Mason, who successfully treated a 15-year-old boy who he believed had warts with hypnosis alone. Dr Mason had successfully treated wart patients with hypnosis in the past and had no reason to believe it would not work with this patient. However, the boy didn't actually have warts. Dr. Mason just thought he did. The truth was that the boy had a far more serious and potentially deadly skin disease known as congenital ichthyosis, a disease that makes the skin leathery.

Dr. Mason successfully treated the boy with only the power of the human mind, and this shocked the medical community. More patients with skin conditions were sent to Dr. Mason, yet he was unable to cure them of their diseases.

After several unsuccessful attempts, the doctor realized why he was unable to help subsequent patients. He acknowledged that, with the successful treatment, he did not know the proper diagnosis but truly believed he could cure the patient, and the patient also believed in his treatment. However, the future treatments failed simply because he admitted that he did not believe hypnosis would succeed in treating the disorder. And doubt nullified the doctor's effectiveness.

This phenomenon helps explain faith healing and other primitive treatments that have documented success.

KEY TAKEAWAY

Your mind can make you sick, and your mind can heal you.

Tubby Smith believed in this same approach to injury prevention, and his athletes believed in him. That's why it worked. The unconscious mind, or what you truly believe is true, determines what the body does and can do. The conscious mind can only sit, observe, think, and worry.

If you're still a bit skeptical of all this so-called psychobabble, consider the following: Dr. Daniel Amen, a well-known child and adult psychiatrist who has done extensive work in evaluating psychiatric and neurological patients with the help of brain imaging, says there is nothing more important to your health—and, ultimately, your life—than what you believe to be true. But the question remains: How can the mind override the body and the genetic makeup that we all inherit at birth?

The answer is found in physics.

The Role of Physics

Modern physics has demonstrated that matter and energy are the same. We think of the mind as energy and the body as matter, but quantum physics has taught us that matter is made up of energy. A piece of steel is essentially energy that is being held very tightly together.

Thoughts (the brain's energy) directly impact the physical brain, which, in turn, controls the functions of the body. Through modern science, we now know that thought-energy can activate or inhibit physical functionality on a cellular level.

Everyone who took Psychology 101 in college remembers the story of Pavlov's dogs and the theory of conditioning. In short, Pavlov was studying the digestion of dogs in a laboratory. (Like Freud, he did not begin his career as a psychologist.) Every day, the dogs were fed, and every day, they heard the sound of a bell when their caretaker came through the door to feed them. The dogs learned to associate the sound of the bell with food. As soon as they heard the bell, they began to salivate in anticipation of food.

The takeaway from the research is that learning and behavioral changes can take place at an unconscious or unintentional level. Unconscious learning leads to unconscious behavioral changes, which in turn lead to the creation of unconscious habits. Most of the habitual behaviors we exhibit today were not acquired through a deliberate and intentional process. Even simple nervous habits like biting our nails or touching our faces when talking were brought about by unconscious beliefs that came from some unconscious lesson we learned along the way.

The good news is that it is always possible to develop new habits or change old, unconscious ones through the use of the conscious mind, which is deliberate and intentional. This point is the major thrust of this book.

In fact, if I were to summarize the primary difference between elite competitors and those who are not, it is that elite competitors make it their business to understand and manage their unconscious minds by mastering their conscious thoughts and behavior. Simply put, they outperform others because they have trained themselves to believe, think, and behave in optimal unison.

Most scientists who focus on the relationship between unconscious beliefs and behavior believe that the unconscious mind is in control of the human body 90 to 95 percent of the time. I'm not sure how one comes to such conclusions, and, frankly, I don't think it matters if the unconscious mind is in control 50 percent or 95 percent of the time. The important thing to realize is that if you are in the business of changing behavior and improving performance, you must understand that your unconscious mind plays a major role in what we call "success," "performance," "excellence," or "greatness." And if you can learn to manage your unconscious mind, you can learn to master your performance in any physical endeavor.

KEY TAKEAWAY

Most people don't choose their habits. Successful people bring conscious thinking to a mostly unconscious process.

The Power of the Conscious

Now that I've demonstrated how powerful the unconscious mind is and how it tends to dominate our behavior, I want to remind you to not give up on the underdog—the conscious mind. It is also powerful and has the ability to move mountains.

Free will, drive, determination, and motivation are all by-products of the conscious mind. The good news is that the conscious mind has the capacity to override the unconscious mind. The keyword here is "capacity." Sadly, most of us do not take advantage of this ability and instead function on autopilot.

Most of the things we learn and accept as truth take place at the unconscious level. Even if the information is false or inaccurate, it is accepted at the unconscious level as truth.

Let's look at an example. If you repeatedly tell a young child that she is smart, she will believe you. How does she even know what smart is? She probably doesn't, but she believes she is regardless. Likewise, if a father continually tells his son that he is lazy, the son will adopt that belief of himself as well. This is what social psychologists refer to as the Looking Glass Phenomenon. Children adopt the beliefs of their parents and other significant others because they are not born with a belief system. They adopt a particular belief system most of the time without even noticing.

Every adult I have ever met has very strong beliefs about who they are and what they are capable of. Although a small percentage over-exaggerate their skills and abilities, the vast majority of us underestimate our power and impact. You believe you do certain things well but not others. You believe you have specific skills and talents and that you are not talented in other areas. To see one's self clearly, we must begin to look at our beliefs more critically. We must look for the proof and evidence. And, when there is no evidence, we must have the courage to admit we are wrong about ourselves.

You adopted a belief system too, but do you know whose beliefs you adopted? To gain more insight into this, I suggest that you actually write down your belief system so that you can get a good look at it. Do this by simply listing all of the things you believe are true. This will take many pages and several days to complete.

The conclusion most insightful and aware people come to after completing this exercise is that the majority of their belief system has no objective data to support it. In other words, most of our beliefs are based on a subjective set of beliefs that ignore many of our subsequent experiences. Once you become aware of how insignificant many of the things are that you hold strongly to, you then allow yourself to start letting them go, and then you are able to see the world more clearly, without the lens of your subjective beliefs.

Beliefs in the Real World

People strongly believe that their beliefs are valid simply because they believe them. Unfortunately, this is not true, and the false beliefs that we hold limit our lives in significant ways.

Instead of always standing firm in our beliefs, what we should be doing in order to grow is *challenging* our beliefs. But this proves to be very hard to do when most of the institutions in our world are designed to support and reinforce a previously held set of beliefs.

Think of it this way: Religious institutions are constantly trying to get us to adopt their views on God and how God wants us to behave. Governments are creating laws and rules that they insist we accept, even if they are unjust and ultimately hurtful to the people who are governed. Educational institutions believe they have the truth via science and we must give the answer the professor wants to hear or we will fail to advance.

While all of this may seem daunting, we are fortunate enough to live in a time when challenging previously held views and beliefs is more common, even if the results are both pain and progress.

Beliefs in Action

Each of us holds beliefs about what we do well and what we don't do well. The fact of the matter is you cannot separate the belief from the ability because they are connected. The primary reason you don't do something well is because you believe it is difficult, impossible, or not very enjoyable.

Athletes I have worked with can tell me the strengths and weaknesses of their game, but what I want them to understand is the relationship between their beliefs and their actual performance. Once the belief changes from "I can't do this very well" to "I think I can do this if I change," then the actual behaviors and outcomes change. The beliefs that you have about yourself and your abilities are not facts. They are your tightly held opinions. In other words, it's really not primarily about your ability. It's what you *believe* about your ability that shapes your potential success.

When I work with distance runners, I love to ask them this question: "If you started running now at a very slow to moderate pace, how far do you think you could go before you passed out from exhaustion?" The fact of the matter is none of them have ever tried this, so they don't really know. However, when I suggest that they could run all day and into the night, a debate usually breaks out. It would be in the athlete's best interest to say, "I'm not really sure, but I bet I would surprise myself." And this is true. When you let go of some of your strongly held and limiting beliefs, I promise you that you will surprise yourself.

Preparing Your Unconscious Mind

Your mind is incredibly fast. It processes information at a speed you cannot even imagine. Once you see an object, it takes your brain about a half-second to generate an emotional response. That's how fast the unconscious mind works. And seeing only represents one-fifth of the ways in which your brain receives information. When you also consider the constant streams of information coming from what you are hearing, tasting, touching, and smelling, it's easy to see how habits—including habitual beliefs—are formed without a conscious thought.

There is simply no time to use the conscious mind to think about something if the unconscious mind works that fast on that much information simultaneously. Therefore, to improve our behavior and ultimately our performance, we must get our unconscious minds wired and ready for success *before* events happen. This is where mental practice, imagery, self-talk, and other techniques come into play and become very valuable tools.

Everyone practices some form of self-deception because we all believe things that are not true and yet we have no idea that our beliefs are inaccurate. Once we internalize a belief, it becomes part of our brain's operating system, similar to how a virus infects a computer. You didn't want it and may not have known when the virus (a false belief) entered the system, but now that it's in, it's very difficult to get rid of it.

KEY TAKEAWAY

We do what we think we can do. We don't attempt
what we think we are incapable of.

Your current performance, whether you are an employee or an athlete, is the sum of your belief system, which is subconscious (that is, it is made up of beliefs you do not actively think about whether or not you know the basis of those beliefs). Great bosses and coaches affect the belief system of their subordinates via the conscious process. This too is where you can begin if you want to be your own best boss or coach.

My 17-year-old daughter, Kate, is quite a good distance runner. She knows I work with professional runners, but that doesn't get me any points with her. As the old adage goes, "No man can be a prophet in his own town" and certainly not in his own home.

However, during the cross-country season of her sophomore year, I bought her a pair of compression socks. We were driving to her race one Saturday morning, and I suggested she try the socks for the first time during her race that day.

"Do you think it will help?" she asked.

"Absolutely," I said. "I bet you will run at least a minute faster than you normally do if you wear the socks. Your legs will feel lighter and fresher."

Surprisingly, she took my advice and wore the socks. Not surprisingly, she ran the fastest race of her life and broke the 19-minute barrier in a 5K cross-country event for the first time ever. Her teammates were amazed by her improved performance, and soon they all wanted to know where they could get a pair of the socks.

The following week at the next race, not only did all of the girls have on compression socks but they also bought the same brand and color. This is a powerful example of what psychologists refer to as the *placebo effect*. A placebo has no true medical, chemical, or physical benefits. However, placebos are extremely effective because of the effect they have on the mind of the individual using them.

KEY TAKEAWAY

Whatever you believe is true, is.

The Placebo Effect

Modern medicine has disassociated itself from the benefits of placebos primarily because there is not much money to be made selling sugar pills. But the placebo effect is not only observed with drugs. It is also observed with surgery.

The *New England Journal of Medicine* published an article in 2002 that described an experiment in which the placebo effect was tested in surgery. The lead author noted in the article that "all good surgeons know there is no placebo effect in surgery," yet he had the courage to test that assumption.

Subjects were placed into one of three groups. Group 1 had the damaged cartilage in their knees shaved away. Group 2 had their knee joints flushed out with a solution and had tissue removed that was believed to be causing the arthritis. Both of these two surgeries were the standard treatment at the time for an arthritic knee. Group 3—the placebo group—was sedated for surgery, and three small incisions were made, but no actual surgery took place.

What do you think were the results of the study? There was no significant difference between the three groups. But that's not the surprising news. What is even more amazing to me is that findings like these are all but ignored by the medical community, including doctors, hospitals, insurance companies, and pharmaceutical companies. As a rule, they don't like the fact that the placebo effect is real because it's terrible for business!

It certainly got my attention, as I have had this exact surgery on both of my knees.

Think about how many products are on the market today that don't benefit the consumer one bit. Now think about how many products are on the market today that not only don't help but are proven to do *harm* to the consumer. Last time I checked, the tobacco companies were doing just fine.

The Nocebo Effect

You can't talk about the placebo effect without mentioning the *nocebo effect* (the power of negative beliefs). In 1961, Walter Kennedy coined the term "nocebo," which in Latin means "I will harm." (The term *placebo* in Latin means "I will please.") The power of the negative nocebo is just as awesome as the power of the positive placebo. Unfortunately, it appears that there is more nocebo than placebo going on these days.

In experimental conditions, the placebo and the nocebo effects can be the same. The only difference is what the doctor and patient believe the agent will elicit before the treatment phase has begun. With the placebos, the most powerful responses occur when both the doctor and patient believe the placebo will work. The same is true with the nocebo. When both parties believe something will be damaging, it usually is. (The next time you buy a voodoo doll and stick needles in it, make sure the person you are casting your spell upon knows what you are doing and believes in the ill effects of such a spell.)

Our unconscious and conscious belief systems not only affect our health, behavior, habits, and performance but they also determine our quality of life. The concept of confidence has received a tremendous amount of attention in both the sports and business arenas. Confidence is just another way to describe our belief systems.

Every time I hear individuals say, "I feel confident," I ask them if confidence is a feeling or a thought. Most think of it as an emotion. Confidence at an unconscious level may seem like an emotion because of the individual's sense of being controlled by the belief. However, once you become conscious of confidence, you quickly realize that confidence is a thought, not an emotion.

In order to help individuals improve their confidence, you have to work at the conscious level and address it as a thought. As long as individuals with low confidence view the belief or thought as a feeling, they will never be able to change their condition. But once individuals with low confidence understand that they have negative and false beliefs about themselves and their abilities, you can begin to help them create a new belief system and a higher self-confidence.

The Relationship Between Cognitions, Emotions, and Behavior

Another way to view this is to examine the relationship between cognitions, emotions, and behavior. The majority of people who seek the professional help of a psychologist or psychiatrist do so because they want to *feel* differently. The vast majority of these patients suffer from either depression or anxiety, and if you have one, you usually have both.

With my master's and doctorate degrees, I worked for several years as a psychotherapist. I spent time in both outpatient and inpatient facilities. Teenagers usually ended up in treatment because of their *behavior*. They were not unsatisfied with how they felt, but their parents were certainly unhappy with how they behaved. Adults, on the other hand, usually came to treatment primarily because of how they felt. There were frequently behavioral concerns, but it was emotional distress that initially got them into treatment. Yet, of all the people I treated over those years, I cannot remember anyone coming into treatment asking me to help them change the way they thought or to alter their belief system. They wanted to feel and behave differently, but they didn't want to give up the inaccurate belief system that was at the root of their troubles.

Good therapies and most religions have something in common: the search for the truth. Once the quest for the truth is replaced with a desire to feel good, the journey is over. The search for truth is a cognitive process that requires both the conscious and unconscious mind in order to succeed.

As Dr. Lipton so clearly states, "Beliefs control biology." I would make a small amendment to that. Beliefs control biology, biology controls behavior, and behavior determines success.

KEY TAKEAWAY

In the battle of mind versus body, mind always wins!

Consider this: What if you suffer from a case of mistaken identity? Who you *think* you are is not actually who you are. What you *think* you are here to do is not actually what you are here to do. What you *think* you are capable of is actually only a hint of your true ability.

Consider for a moment that you are totally wrong about yourself—and wrong about this infinite universe in which you live. What if that's true? What if most of us live our entire lives and never know who we actually are, why we are here, and what we are supposed to do while visiting this planet? What if we have amnesia and we forgot who we really are right before we left our mother's body and entered the world? I think this is exactly our state.

Who we think we are is not who we are. We are much, much more than our perceived selves.

The Buddhists have a saying: "Don't mistake the finger pointing to the moon for the moon itself." We think our ego—our persona—is who we really are. But this is only to the same extent that your clothes, your hairstyle, and your personality are who you are. In order to reach your full potential—your greatness—you must first admit that you are wrong about yourself.

2

•————————•

Beliefs and Behaviors

There are three kinds of men. The ones that learn by reading.
The few who learn by observation. The rest of them have
to pee on the electric fence themselves.

—WILL ROGERS

Belief is unconscious—it's where what we hold true about ourselves resides. This is also our source of emotion. Though we do not consciously choose our emotional response to events, our emotional response is ultimately dictated by our belief system.

If your emotions are in charge, you will never fully know yourself, and you will never reach your potential in a performance environment. That said, the best way to improve your emotional state is to first examine and correct your belief system.

Beliefs, Thoughts, and Behaviors

There are three primary components necessary to improve performance: beliefs, thoughts, and behaviors.

Beliefs

Beliefs are absolutely critical to performance, and ultimately they determine how well you will perform. The question is: *Where do our beliefs come from?* How do we come to believe what we hold as truth?

Initially, we all adopt our beliefs from others. For example, during childhood, you probably adopted the beliefs of your parents and other significant people in your life. Think about this for a moment: One of the most important dictators of your performance was not determined by you. Instead, someone else set your life on its current trajectory.

If the people from whom you adopted your self-beliefs did a good and accurate job of telling you the truth about who you really are, consider yourself one of the lucky ones. But what if they were wrong? What if they failed to see your potential, abilities, and talents? Then what? Well, that's where the problem starts.

We have all adopted some accurate and some inaccurate beliefs. The trouble is most of us don't know which is which:

Belief: I am not a good person. My coach doesn't care
              about me.
Thought: I don't want to be on this team, and I don't want to
              train today.
Behavior: Poor performance.

• ———— •

Belief: I am a good person. My coach is a good coach.
Thought: I am going to do whatever my coach tells me to do. I
              trust her.
Behavior: High performance.

Thoughts

Thoughts are conscious. Our thoughts are usually a by-product of our beliefs, but it is possible to have a thought that is inconsistent with your beliefs. You can "think" something you don't believe is true.

For example, most people believe there is some aspect about themselves that is not "okay"—there's something they need to improve about themselves. However, when someone else comments on this particular issue or points out the need for improvement, their unconscious response is typically to become hurt or angry even though they fundamentally agree.

Thoughts are easier to change than beliefs, so you should put most of your energy toward improving your thinking. Ultimately, you can change your unconscious beliefs through conscious thought.

Behaviors

Behaviors are what we do. It is very difficult to change long-term behaviors, but less difficult to change short-term behaviors. A long-term behavior is known as a *habit*, while a short-term behavior is known as an *action*. Taking action on a regular basis ultimately leads to a change in habit.

A change to any one of your beliefs, thoughts, or behaviors will have an effect on the other two. When all three are aligned, performance is maximized. But most people do not have all three aligned and therefore experience some internal struggle or frustration, and their performance is hindered as a result.

Are You Changing?

How will you know if you are effectively changing your beliefs, thoughts, or behaviors? There is a simple litmus test. You will know that you are successfully changing any one of these when you feel very uncomfortable with yourself and, potentially, with others. You may even experience pain and mental anguish during the process. In fact, more pain is usually associated with greater change and improvement.

KEY TAKEAWAY

Unfortunately, "No pain, no gain" is mostly a true statement.

When we find a bug or error in our belief system, we usually install a "belief patch" to cover up the immediate issue, but we don't typically go back and do the hard work of bringing the entire belief into question. For most of us, that would be way too scary and unsettling.

But, if you strive for greatness, that's exactly what you must do. You have to throw the whole thing out and start again from scratch.

Because it is easier to change what we think, we often alter our thoughts rather than change our behaviors and habits. Most of us have false beliefs about ourselves that limit our performance and at the same time keep us from making the necessary behavioral changes. Here's an example:

At some point in their career, most athletes believe that they are talented and among the best in their sport at that given level. They believe that their talent is the primary reason they are good and that their training habits have only a secondary effect on their performance.

The vast majority of really good high school athletes who go on to earn college scholarships fall into this category. They were one of the best kids on their team all through Little League and high school. Sure, they trained and practiced hard, but no more than the other athletes they competed with in high school. Eventually, they develop the belief that they can be better than their competitors with the same amount of effort.

Then they go to college where everyone is talented. They quickly go from being the best athlete on the team to not even playing. They are frequently red-shirted so that they can have another year of development before using up their four years of eligibility. This creates a real problem for most of these athletes, and the same cycle might happen again if they make it to the pros.

When most athletes advance to a higher level of play, their beliefs about themselves are usually affected. It's harder to believe you are really good when the talent level increases.

The belief change that college athletes must make is to begin believing that they will be successful—not so much because of physical talent but because of their work ethic, discipline, knowledge of the game, coachability, and desire to improve. But if they never thought those things were important before, changing their viewpoint can be difficult.

This is a condition I refer to as the "curse of talent." The best athletes change their beliefs about what will make them better once they get to college, while those who never change their belief systems will never make it in college sports.

Changing your belief system means you must admit that what you previously believed was wrong or is no longer true. If the belief changes, there can then be a change in behavior. No change in belief equals no change in behavior.

Most of the time when we change our minds, we substitute one false belief for another. This type of belief change does not lead to improvement. But when we substitute a *truth* for a false belief, this does likely lead to an increase in performance.

When belief and thought are not aligned, we call this *cognitive dissonance*. The lack of alignment causes some internal tension and poor performance. When belief and behavior are not aligned, we will again experience tension. And when thought and behavior are not aligned, again the results are tension and poor performance.

The ideal scenario, which is one that creates the highest level of performance, is when belief, thought, and behavior are all aligned. For example, when an athlete believes she is talented and has great potential, that is her truth. She thinks, "I am going to work hard to develop my potential because being talented alone will not make me a great competitor." As a result, she changes her behavior. She goes out every day and works hard.

Learning is basically a relentless pursuit of the truth, and this quest will keep you curious and actively engaged throughout your life.

Most great learners are lifelong learners. They never stop being curious. As Einstein once described himself, "I have no special talent. I am only passionately curious."

The problem with most performance environments is the assumption that everyone wants to learn, improve, and reach their potential. Unfortunately, this is not the case. What most people want is for you to tell them that everything is okay—that they are fine just the way they are.

This is why you see most people become quite defensive or hurt when someone tells them that they are not performing well or that they need to improve. Those comments disrupt the person's happiness or peace of mind and the belief that they are "doing just fine."

But what about *un-learning*?

It is quite possible that un-learning would be much more beneficial to many of us than learning. It has been my observation that the primary barrier to many people's success is not necessarily a lack of knowledge; instead, it is all of the stuff they know, or their false beliefs.

Think about it: One of the most frustrating experiences we frequently have is dealing with a "know-it-all."

I experienced this early in my career. I discovered that many coaches believed they should be a sport psychologist as well as a coach.

They pretended to know what they were doing, even when their deception worked to the detriment of their athletes. Parents could also have the same effect. Have you ever observed an incompetent parent ruin a perfectly good child? I have.

What we have learned, or what we believe is true, is among our greatest hurdles. Some of what you believe is true, but the rest isn't. The issue is that we just don't know the difference. Ultimately, it's better to *not* know. Not knowing leads to curiosity, whereas knowing leads to contentment and arrogance—neither of which will increase your performance.

The Truth About Self-Deception

For the small percentage of you who really want to improve and reach your full potential, read on. The rest of you should skip ahead to the next chapter because it's about to get ugly.

Still in? Good!

In order to discover the truth about yourself, you must first accept that all humans participate in some level of self-deception. We all lie to ourselves. We do this not because we are bad people but because we are, well, *people*. There are certain truths about ourselves that are too unsettling to acknowledge, so we massage the truth into a belief that we can live with.

There are also the things that the grown-ups around us tell us about ourselves that are inaccurate but that we believe anyway. Children are inherently trusting and adopt the beliefs of their parents, teachers, and family. But, as we said before, parents and coaches sometimes have false or limiting beliefs and they may have gotten those beliefs—or at least some of them—wrong. What if, despite all of their good intentions, they simply don't know the truth?

As I explained earlier, social psychology offers a construct called the Looking Glass Phenomenon, which basically states that a child

29

looks to his or her immediate surroundings (family, school, and so on) to develop a self-image and other core beliefs.

Are you beginning to see how this can get ugly in a hurry?

As adults who are actively pursuing our full potential, we must go back and revisit all of the things we took at face value as a kid. We must make a list of all of the things we think are true and then ask ourselves, "How do I know this is true? What evidence do I have to demonstrate this truth?"

This is a lengthy and difficult process, but it leads to a tremendous amount of insight and discovery. As you work through your list, you will discover that some of your beliefs or truths have little to no supporting data while others do. Yet continue to ask yourself, "What is true, and how do I know it is true?"

Once you become comfortable with this process, you will be surprised at what you keep and what you discard. If you are diligent with the exercise, you will find yourself dismissing more "truths" than you keep.

Once you have become proficient at telling yourself the truth, you are then in a place where you can speak candidly and honestly to others. This skill is especially beneficial to people in leadership roles (managers, coaches, parents, and teachers). You cannot help a person improve without the ability to speak truthfully.

This means sometimes sharing an opinion or observation that is different from that of others. Differences in opinion often lead to interpersonal tension or crisis, something most people want to avoid. However, it is impossible to improve and develop without a clear sense of what is true and what is not. Each of us has beliefs that benefit us and others that hinder us. All of us exhibit behaviors that are both constructive and destructive.

Getting past the desire to be "special" or perfect is absolutely necessary for your growth and improvement. Many of us believe we must be special in order to be okay. If we were to think of ourselves as "average" or "normal," we would become very distraught or depressed.

Believing that you can be normal and also achieve greatness is the truth many of us have yet to realize. Your normality— or your realization that you have more in common with others than not—is what will allow you to make sense of your struggles and failures.

Essentially, you need to get over yourself. The less time you spend thinking about yourself, the more time you have to focus on what it is you want to do—and the better off you will be. Performance increases as one's obsession and concern for one's self decreases. We don't fail because there is something wrong with us. We fail because we are human.

The human design is not perfect, and it allows for a lot of variation; thus our performance varies from day to day. Learn to accept this truth and you will be much happier, and your overall performance will improve.

Imagine working in an environment where everyone is passionately pursuing the truth about themselves—a place where there is very little ego and quite a bit of humility. These types of environments are almost nonexistent. However, this should be our ultimate goal. The best teams and best businesses have this type of environment.

Performance does not take place in a vacuum. All performance is influenced by the environment because humans are social animals. We live in tribes, families, and communities.

When a group of people has become adept at telling themselves the truth, they will automatically begin telling each other the truth. In business environments, we call this *feedback*. In sport, we call it *coaching*.

My observation has been that there is very little truth telling in corporate America. In fact, telling the truth is the most dangerous thing one can do in most business and social settings. Most veterans of the corporate world have at least one story of how they went to their boss or colleague, took a risk and shared an honest opinion, and were later penalized for their honesty.

KEY TAKEAWAY

Most people tell lies primarily because it is too dangerous
to tell the truth—not because of some character
defect. Great leaders make it safe for others
to tell the truth and then reward that behavior.

Fortunately, leaders of athletic teams are frequently better truth tellers than corporate leaders because there is more objectivity and transparency in sport than business. In sport, you have the concept of *practice*, where it is expected that one will make mistakes while trying to develop a skill or improve.

Business has not yet incorporated the concept of practice into its milieu. Every meeting and conversation is a game, not practice. Every day is game day. This makes mistakes much more costly, and it also increases the chance that the same mistake will be repeated.

Now, some business folks may take exception to this concept and say, "We have training programs, and that is similar to practice." Well, I'm quite familiar with the training concept in business, which is very similar to our unimpressive educational system. Both corporate and educational systems are very didactic, focusing on reading and listening instead of experimenting and doing. Success is defined by memorizing the right answer and obtaining more knowledge. That system is not effective in bringing about changes in behavior.

Imagine for a minute that you need a surgery that is somewhat complex, but it has only been performed successfully by a handful of doctors for a couple of years. Now, I want you to pick a surgeon. Here are your choices:

- *Surgeon 1* is a well-respected professor who has written extensively and read everything that has ever been written about your condition and the surgical procedure that you need to have performed, but he has never actually performed the surgery.

- *Surgeon 2* is a practicing surgeon who spends most of her time in the hospital treating patients and performing the surgery that you need. She has performed the surgery many times, and her success rate is high. She does not teach, she does not lecture, and when she gets home, she is too tired to read.

Which would you pick? The one with experience, right? In a performance environment, experience is more valuable than information.

Practice allows for failure, even encourages it—that is, if you take the right approach. If you want to create an environment where performance improves, you must first make it safe to fail. That's as true for your individual practices as it is for team practice. Those who are free to admit they fell short can get better. And if you can laugh at yourself when you struggle, feel some discomfort, or suffer downright pain, you can get better. Pain is when the real improvement kicks in.

3

•————————————•

Better Is the Enemy of Best

To find yourself, think for yourself.

—SOCRATES

We live in a culture that is obsessed with "better." No matter what we have or how well we are doing, we want *better*. Furthermore, we passionately believe that the desire to do better or have more is critical to actually being successful. We blindly embrace the mantra "You have to want it to get it," but we should also acknowledge that relatively few people have actually put this to the test. Think about it this way: Do we actually get better because of our desire to improve? Or are our actual growth and development caused by something other than this desire for better?

Additionally, we have a grave concern that if we ever become happy with our current status, then we will somehow lose our edge and plummet into mediocrity. Because of this, most of us are taught to never be content with where we are and to always strive to be better. Our obsession with *better* can be heard before every practice—"Let's be better today"—and in every performance review in corporate America— "We need to see better numbers before we can promote you."

The paradox of our rising desires and expectations is that as we want and get more money, better services, and increased luxuries, the quality of our life doesn't actually increase. We are not getting happier as we strive to be more successful. Instead, statistics suggest we are actually going backward.

How do we stop this trend of going in reverse? We replace better with best.

Replacing Better with Best

If we decide to let *better* go, what do we replace it with? I recommend we pursue our *best*, instead of *better*. The problem with *better* is that it's a subjective judgment. When someone tells you that you can or should do better, you are not encouraged by that critic. Instead, you feel judged. Additionally, when we tell ourselves we should do better, we are also critiquing ourselves, judging ourselves as not enough.

This type of judgment is not helpful when growing and developing skills. I frequently ask the groups I speak with to think of the best career advice they ever received. Once they have identified an answer, I ask them to categorize the statement into either an encouragement or a criticism. Consistently, the vast majority of the group reports the best advice they ever received came in the form of an encouragement.

Better is a criticism; *best* is an encouragement.

What most of us desperately need is not to get better and tell ourselves we aren't good enough. Instead we need to tell ourselves to do the best we can and that will be enough.

Your Best Is Good Enough

Humans have one of two fundament beliefs about themselves. I ask my clients to tell me which of these two statements more accurately portrays how they talk to themselves:

1. I need to get better.
2. I am good enough now.

The vast majority of us say the first statement: "I need to get better." Interestingly, it doesn't matter how successful we've become—most of us want to get better. Yet the reason we want to get better is our belief that we are not yet good enough.

Growth is a natural process and happens whether we desire it or not, but the belief that one needs to be better actually hinders this process. Our consistent criticism and failure to make peace with who we are **now** has very detrimental effects on both mind and body.

Most of the athletes I work with arrive quickly at the idea that they need to get better, and they believe that their mind is getting in the way. While I may agree, I also suggest that the belief that they need to be better or be something other than what they currently are, is also limiting them. I ask them to tell me about a time when they performed at their absolute best. Everyone can do this, even though some may struggle initially. Once they begin to tell their story of their best, they talk about how easy it was, how there was no resistance, and how there was nothing to struggle with or fight against. I then ask, "If you could access your best more frequently, would you stop being obsessed with getting better?" Their answer is always along the lines of, "Well, of course." The secret here is that you cannot pursue both *better* and *best*. You have to pick one. As long as you are adamantly pursuing *better*, you will not find your *best*.

WHEN ARE WE AT OUR BEST?

Viktor Frankl, a Holocaust survivor and Austrian-trained psychiatrist, summarized this struggle eloquently in his book, published in 1959, *Man's Search for Meaning*. Dr. Frankl warns us against pursuing success and happiness:

continued

Don't aim at success—the more you aim at it and make it a target, the more you are going to miss it. For success, like happiness, cannot be pursued; it must ensue, and it only does so as the unintended side-effect of one's personal dedication to a course greater than oneself. Happiness must happen, and the same holds true for success: you have to let it happen by not caring about it. I want you to listen to what your conscience commands you to do and go on to carry it out to the best of your knowledge. Then you will live to see that in the long-run—in the long-run, I say!—success will follow you precisely because you had forgotten to think about it.

I believe that we are at our best when we are not even considering ourselves in life. During my best days, I don't even think about or consider myself because I'm too busy working and helping other people. My worst days are those when I sit around and contemplate how things are going for me. I immediately think of the things I should be doing or the things I have already done but did not do well enough. Alternatively, when we reflect upon a job well done or a challenge to overcome, it is then that we are most fully alive. Therefore, instead of pursuing happiness and success, we should actually be hunting for our next big challenge, our next impossible feat. Or as Frankl once wrote: "Those who have a 'why' to live, can bear with almost any 'how.'"

I recently met with one of the top collegiate tennis programs in the country. The team has won multiple conference and national championships. The coach is recognized as one of the best coaches in collegiate tennis. At the time of our meeting, the team was ranked in the top 20 in the country, and the best player was ranked no. 3 in the country.

The team, which consisted of 10 athletes and 3 coaches, was crowded in a tightly cramped locker room as I began a 30-minute presentation.

"I want you all to think about the last time you walked off the court after a match and thought to yourself, 'I just played the best tennis I am capable of playing,'" I began. I gave them a few moments to think about the question. Then, I told them to think about when it was, whom they were playing, and why they thought they had played to the best of their ability and to raise their hand once they identified the moment.

We went around the room, and only 2 of the 10 athletes talked about a recent match. The remaining 8 players stated it had been at least a year since they had played their best, and one athlete stated it had been 3 years since he had played his best.

Remember, these are elite athletes. They play tennis almost every day of their lives, for several hours, and it is the central fixture of their lives.

Just imagine how frustrating it must be to spend such an inordinate amount of time doing something you love but not be able to do your best.

The Relationship with and Need for Struggle

Most of us tend to think of the events of our lives as either good or bad, pleasurable or painful. Unfortunately, this type of compartmentalization does not actually help us understand how to grow and develop new skills. In fact, we *need* the bad times in order to have the good. There is no great performance without the failures. There is no optimal performance without the stress and struggle of trying something we cannot yet do.

Steven Kotler, author of *The Rise of Superman,* gathered research on optimal performance and described the four stages of entering into optimal performance: struggle, release, flow, and recovery.

Stage 1. Struggle

In order to reach flow, we must begin by trying to do something we cannot do well or easily. In business, this may be developing a new product or process that is superior to our current one. In sport, we may begin the season by training harder and longer than we did prior to the season.

This struggle creates a significant change in our brain chemistry. We become more focused and intense because of the release of stress hormones (norepinephrine, cortisol, and adrenaline). Yet we can't release the hormones until we stress the system. Unfortunately, this stress leads to frustration and anger in most of us, which in turns leads many of us to disengage or quit. How we handle this critical period dictates whether or not we will advance or stay stuck in our frustration. Those who don't lose hope but, rather, see the benefit of this crucial period will have a huge advantage over their competitors because they will find their best more frequently.

Stage 2. Release

The second stage is the period between struggle and flow. Release takes place when we back away from the challenge and allow ourselves time to recover. When we do this, the stress hormones found in the first stage dissipate.

How we go about entering into release is not important—there are numerous ways to initiate this stage. Doing something less serious or playful will usually work. Laughter is a sign that release has begun. Once we release, another chemical change takes place in the brain: nitric oxide pours into the synapses of the brain. Nitric oxide acts as a precursor to the beneficial chemicals associated with Flow (dopamine and endorphins).

Stage 3. Flow

The two earlier stages are absolutely essential to establishing the foundation for flow, and flow is the foundation for your being your best. In other words, stress followed by laughter leads to the aha! feeling. If you're a mathematician, then: struggle + fun = awesome.

Stage 4. Recovery

After we experience the wonders of flow, we must go through a period of recovery. Flow, although incredible, is also very taxing to the human mind. It requires tremendous amounts of energy and neurochemistry.

One of the most beneficial aspects of recovery is memory consolidation, during which data is moved from short-term memory to long-term storage. This process allows us to keep the experience we just had with us and is beneficial to increasing our self-efficacy and confidence for future events. However, entering into recovery is like coming down from the mountain top experience of flow—it's a bit of a bummer. We no longer feel high and expansive. We are once again human.

Beliefs About the Future

In addition to the beliefs we have about self, we also have a fundamental belief about the future and what will happen to us.

Most of us believe one of two things:

1. It will be okay.
2. It will not be okay.

As you might imagine, our belief about the future has a tremendous impact on how we live our lives and perform in the present. If we believe things are going to be okay, then we will experience much less stress, anxiety, depression, addiction, and sleeplessness than if we believe the alternative. In sports, the athlete who believes he or she will play well and be victorious can focus on the game at hand and not be anxious or tight as the game progresses. In business, the confident sales representative who believes the client will want to purchase the product is able to give an informed and confident sales presentation.

When I speak to sales teams, I tell them that before they even meet with or speak to a client, they have subconsciously been thinking about the call and how it's going to play out. They either believe that the customer is going to do business with them or not do business with them. This belief leads to behaviors that we are sometimes not even aware of. Many of our responses and reactions during a conversation are beyond our conscious awareness. Therefore, confident sales reps have a huge competitive advantage over sales reps who don't think they can make the sale. By believing that the prospect will become a client, they increase their chances of actually gaining the business.

A negative belief about the future almost always leads to anxiety and stress. In fact, that is what anxiety or worry is—a negative belief about the future. Anxiety is future based, while depression is past based. If you ask people what they are anxious about, they will tell you a story of something they are fearful will happen in the near future. When talking to people who are depressed, their story typically begins with the past and the unfortunate events that they have had to endure.

When we talk about the future, most of us speak of it as if it is a thing, an entity, or a certainty, when that's not what it is at all. The future is a made-up thought that you have created. It is a fictitious story that you have been writing your entire life. Every day you rewrite the story of "My Future." Interestingly, we are not consciously aware that we are creating a fictitious story and acting as if it were nonfiction. We trick ourselves into believing something that is fabricated because our mind doesn't realize we invented it.

The Self-Fulfilling Prophesy

Most of us tend to create a story based on someone else's life or our past life events. In order to become a fully functioning adult, you must understand that your future is primarily determined by what you tell yourself about the future. Have you ever noticed what your mind does when you are preparing to take a trip to a place you have never been before? It creates the place! You don't actually do this with conscious intent. It just happens. As you think about the hotel, your mind creates a hotel. When you think about the climate or what the weather will be like, your mind magically creates that too. If you are going to meet someone there that you have never met before, bam . . . there is the person. You created the entire experience before you even left home.

Now here's the magic. It just so happens that what we think will happen, frequently does. It's known as the Self-Fulfilling Prophesy. The Self-Fulfilling Prophesy states that the beliefs one has about the future can actually dictate behavior in the present, which in turn causes the prediction to become true.

Let's look at an example. I recently worked with Jane Park, a professional golfer on the LPGA tour. While discussing her game, she shared that her driver was her best club and that her putter was her worst. I asked her why she thought she was driving the ball so well. She told me that she knows where the ball is going to go before she hits it. She said, "I just look at my target. I don't have to think about my swing because the ball will go there." In putting, it was just the opposite. She had no confidence that the ball would go where she wanted it to go, and therefore she was preoccupied with her putting stroke. Instead of imagining her ball going in the hole, she was thinking about her swing technique and how hard she should strike the ball. I told her that she was setting herself up to play poorly by believing it would not go well for her. This story proves that it is important to acknowledge when we are setting up a negative self-fulfilling prophesy. If we don't become conscious of it, it will certainty affect our behavior and the outcome.

Another example of the Self-Fulfilling Prophesy in action can be seen in the classic psychological study conducted by Robert Rosenthal in the late 1960s: the Pygmalion Effect. In this study, teachers at an elementary school were told that five students in their class were "academic spurters," or students who learned fast. Because of these superior cognitive abilities, the teachers expected those five students to outperform the other children in the class. These five students were actually chosen at random and were not intellectually superior to the other children. But the results proved otherwise. Those five students actually outperformed their classmates over the course of the year. Why? Because the teachers gave those students extra attention, provided them with more feedback, asked them more questions, and encouraged them more.

Have you ever seen an example of the Pygmalion Effect in real life? If you pay attention, you will see it everywhere you go. In fact, you may even find yourself doing it.

The fact of the matter is that each of us has the power to create our own future by constantly creating and imagining what will happen next. Interestingly, most psychological research suggests that it's not what happens to us that matters most. Instead it's our response to these events. People who are victims believe that events are happening to them. They start a lot of conversations with, "You're not going to believe what happened to me." In contrast, people who are empowered and feel in control of their lives understand that they always have a choice, despite the situation they find themselves in.

Remember: You are in control of your future and in control of the thoughts that help you reach your goals.

4

•————————•

The Importance of Flow

To reach flow, one must be willing to take risks.
The lover must lay bare his soul and risk rejection and
humiliation to enter this state. The athlete must be
willing to risk physical harm, even loss of life, to
enter this state. The artist must be willing to be scorned
and despised by critics and the public and still push on.
And the average person—you and I—must be
willing to fail, look foolish, and fall flat on our
faces should we wish to enter this state.

—NED HALLOWELL,
HARVARD PSYCHIATRIST

A s we discussed in the previous chapter, flow is the third stage in the process of reaching optimal performance. While each stage is important to achieving this state, understanding and creating a state of flow is essential in creating success in business, sports, and life in general.

The Science Behind Flow

So how do we create this for ourselves? The first step is understanding what flow actually is and the science behind this optimal state.

Brain Waves: Beta, Theta, and Gamma

Scientists have researched people at their best for many years. In sport, we have studied the best athletes and the best performances for decades. This science of optimal human performance has taught us quite a few interesting things about how we find our *best*. An entire lexicon has sprouted up as well, and now we refer to optimal performance as being "in the zone" or "in the flow."

We have also learned that the brain is different when it is in the flow versus when we are struggling or exerting an excessive level of effort. When the brain is in its natural state, the brain waves (or activity) are in the beta stage, and when the brain is in a flow state, the brain waves are in either the theta or gamma stage:

- **Beta waves** are present during normal activities. These waves dominate our normal waking state and are apparent when our attention is directed toward cognitive tasks and events outside of ourselves. Beta waves travel fast and are seen when we are attentive, solving problems, and making decisions. Beta waves also dominate when humans are in a heightened state of alertness, under stress, anxious, or restless.
- **Theta waves** appear in adults during meditative, drowsy, or sleepy states but not during the deepest stages of sleep. Theta waves can produce a sense of deep unity with the universe.
- **Gamma waves** have the fastest frequency range, and they sweep the brain from front to back, about 40 times per second. It is

believed that gamma waves are critical for conscious attention, and without them, an individual could slip into a coma. Gamma waves are believed to be associated with bursts of insight and high-level information processing.

If you compare the flow state to the state in which humans are normally functioning, there is quite a difference. Beta waves are present during most of our waking hours and in the first stage of the flow process (struggle). Yet, once you enter into the active flow state, beta waves give way to theta and gamma waves, and this order is critical to the creation of the flow state.

Neurochemicals: Dopamine, Endorphins, and Anandamide

Additionally, when someone is in a state of flow, the chemistry of the brain is different from other states. Dopamine, endorphins, and anandamide are the three neurochemicals that are most associated with flow, and they are critical to happiness and optimal functioning:

- **Dopamine** is released every time you complete a task (that's why it feels good to check your phone and answer a text), and it is critical in reward-motivated behavior. Every time you receive an award, praise, or validation, dopamine levels in the brain increase.
- **Endorphins** are morphine-like substances created by your body. They help to inhibit the transmission of pain signals, and they can also produce feelings of euphoria. When you exercise or stress your body with physical challenges, you release endorphins. The "runner's high" is a by-product of endorphins.

- **Anandamide** was first discovered in 1992, and it was named after the Sanskrit word *ananda*, which means "bliss," "joy," or "delight." This chemical decreases one's pain, suppresses appetite, elevates mood, improves movement control, and enhances memory. One of the major performance benefits of anandamide is that it inhibits our ability to feel afraid, and it may even extinguish our long-term memories of fear.

Your brain function is a by-product of both electrical currents (brain waves) and chemicals. Our ability to perform at optimal levels depends on these two factors. This research also suggests that in order for humans to be at their best, we need to do physically strenuous activities (which release endorphins) and to complete tasks and have a sense of accomplishment (which releases dopamine). In other words, we are hardwired to challenge ourselves and our bodies, and in turn, our bodies reward us.

We cannot be our best self unless we live our life this way. Unfortunately, many try to find a shortcut to the pleasure and enjoyment we get from the flow experience. This helps explain why so many of us use drugs and other substances to feel better. However, when we artificially attempt to create a flow experience, we create more problems to deal with later. When humans enter into flow naturally, not only do they feel great during the experience but they also increase their self-confidence and abilities.

Chemicals: Cortisol and Norepinephrine

Of course, most of us do not spend the majority of our time in the flow state. In fact, it's just the opposite. Americans are an anxious, nervous, and fearful people, and we pay a very steep price for this mental state. When we are threatened or perceive ourselves as being threatened, the brain releases chemicals that hinder our ability to function and eventually harm our bodies. Two chemicals are found to be prevalent in the brain during stress, cortisol and norepinephrine:

- **Cortisol** is a steroid hormone, and it is released when one is under a great deal of stress or when one's blood-glucose levels become low.
- **Norepinephrine** mobilizes the brain and body for action. Levels are low during sleep and then increase when we wake. When we perceive danger, norepinephrine levels are very high, which is key in the fight-or-flight response that helps us function in life-or-death situations.

When we are under stress, the brain releases cortisol and norepinephrine, and our ability to function becomes impaired. Cortisol is beneficial in small doses and in emergency situations. However, when we remain in a state of stress, cortisol impairs our immune system and inhibits the growth and function of bone and muscle. Cortisol also makes the body more sensitive to the effects of norepinephrine, which leads to reduced blood flow to our muscles.

Norepinephrine is initially beneficial to us when we enter athletic competition because it gets our blood pumping and hearts beating faster. But if you can't manage this burst, you will likely start shaking and lose control of your fine motor skills. This is the process that takes place when we say an athlete has "choked."

It is also important to note that during stressful times, we tend to think more, and some people report that they cannot quiet their minds and get relaxed. We know that during flow states, the mind is quiet and functioning exceptionally well. Science has taught us that when the frontal lobes of the brain (where we think and reason) become too activated, that actually impedes the part of the brain that elicits motor behavior. Therefore, thinking is usually not associated with optimal performance.

How Neurochemicals Relate to Flow

Steven Kotler has also explained how the five major neurochemicals involved in flow interact with one another to help us create a mental state that allows the out-of-the-world performances we frequently observe with adventure athletes to happen.

Think of the chemicals in your brain as sending one of two messages. **Excitatory chemicals** tell the brain to do more or keep doing what it is doing. **Inhibitory chemicals** send a signal to either stop or do less of what you are doing. Human performance is a dance between what is going on inside of you and the activity and people you are engaged with outside of you. Peak performance is a wonderful marriage of your internal and external environments.

There are five neurochemicals that play a critical role in flow, and it is important to understand what each does independently *and* how they collectively work together to create the state of flow.

Dopamine is predominant during flow. We experience dopamine emotionally when we are excited, engaged, and curious. Dopamine is released whenever we take risk or encounter and engage with something new or novel. It essentially rewards that behavior, and whenever we complete a task, we also get a boost of dopamine. Mentally, it helps us pay attention and recognize patterns, and it improves our processing of information. Physically, dopamine affects heart rate, blood pressure, and muscle activation, thus playing a key role in the development of physical skills.

Norepinephrine also activates the body by increasing heart rate and respiration, while also triggering a release of glucose into the bloodstream that gives us an energy boost. The brain is a sugar junky that eats only glucose, so norepinephrine helps feed your brain. Norepinephrine is responsible for increased arousal, attention, and ability to manage emotions. It helps us stay focused on the task at hand and keeps us from being distracted by unimportant things.

Endorphins are the third chemical critical to flow. The term literally translates to "internal morphine," and thus we get an incredible high when our brains release endorphins. When engaged in strenuous physical activity, endorphins keep us from feeling pain, and they can substitute pain with pleasure. Research has suggested that endorphins are 100 times more potent than medical-grade morphine.

Anandamide is another feel-good chemical that is released during exercise-induced flow states, and it elevates mood, relieves pain, and inhibits the ability to feel fear. It also assists in cognitive functioning by improving lateral thinking, which allows us to connect unjoined ideas into one whole. The physical effects of anandamide are dilated blood vessels and bronchial tubes, which assist in the ability to take in oxygen.

Serotonin shows up at the end of the flow state. We have long known that serotonin is a critical neurochemical, and its importance can be found in those affected by depression as there is not enough serotonin active in their brains. Not only does serotonin help with depression but it is also believed to help us deal with adversity and challenge. Serotonin encourages us to not give up when we fail and to keep trying. This chemical is also involved in our ability to feel connected to others and experience ourselves as part of a bigger whole or team.

The Eight Major Components of Flow

Leaders in business are constantly challenging their employees to improve their skills and get more done in a shorter period of time. Even though most leaders acknowledge that they want their employees to do their best, they actually create environments that ensure that they will *not* do their best. Stressful work environments block employees from getting into the flow and doing their best work. Research conducted by Gallup suggests that 70 percent of the U.S. workforce is not engaged at work, leaving only 30 percent of the workforce engaged and functioning at a high level of production.

One of the main factors that keep workers from being engaged is their relationship with their bosses. How bosses interact with their employees is critical to employee performance. Another critical factor is the tasks of the job. It is imperative that employees have a job that they can actually perform and one that matches their skill set.

In my opinion, Mihaly Csikszentmihalyi's *Flow* is perhaps the finest book written on optimal performance today. In the book, he outlines "the phenomenology of enjoyment," stating there are eight major components to make a task, such as work, enjoyable and create a space where one can do his or her best.

Mihaly Csikszentmihalyi's *eight major components of flow* are the following:

1. We must believe that we have a chance of completing the work. How many times have you heard someone say, "I can't do this"? As soon as we believe the task is beyond our reach, it's over. At that moment, the task becomes impossible for us.

2. We must be able to concentrate on the task and not be distracted by environmental factors that are not important. If we are unable to concentrate, we can't perform optimally. There are a million things that keep people from being able to concentrate at work, and one of them is the work itself. Trying to accomplish the task (focus on the result) actually distracts us from the task at hand (process). This happens when we focus on the end result or focus on completing the task instead of focusing on just doing the task.

3. We must have clear goals. In order to perform well, we must have a goal in mind and believe it's reachable. Interestingly, if the goal changes—and in corporate America this is a common event—then people will become confused or distracted, and they will lose the ability to perform at their best.

4. We need immediate feedback on our performance. Humans want to know how they are doing at all times. It's critical to their sense of security.

5. There must be a deep and effortless involvement with the work. If the work environment is stressful, then there are too many distractions that keep employees from being able to concentrate on the task at hand.

6. We must feel a sense of control over our actions. Telling people what to do and how to do it is generally not very beneficial after the people have developed the core skills to do the job. Employees prefer to be told what needs to be done and then be allowed to figure out how to meet the challenge.

7. One of the more interesting aspects of optimal performance is that when we are at our best, we have no awareness of ourselves. When we enter into flow, we no longer think or worry about ourselves. We stop wondering if we are good enough or if things are going to work out. Instead, we just do what is in front of us and stay in the present moment.

8. When we enter into flow, how our brain processes sensory data is altered. Our sense of time is distorted, and we see things differently. Specifically, time can be altered either by slowing down or speeding up our perception. Hours can seem like minutes, and seconds can seem like days. As time becomes altered, our power of perception is enhanced. Athletes frequently report that the ball appears to be larger and moving slower, making it easier to see and make contact. During these times, athletes

feel like they are not only in control of themselves but also in control of the entire game, because of the empowerment they feel over time and space.

These eight major components of flow teach us that we need to forget about trying to get better and instead focus on getting ourselves into the flow, which results in our best self. When we experience flow, it leaves us feeling more confident, skilled, and excited. In fact, by doing our best, we actually get better faster and accelerate growth and improvement. When we focus on better, we actually inhibit flow and slow down the developmental process.

5

The Intention of *Why*

What is to give light must endure burning.

—Viktor Frankl

There is a great line in Lewis Carroll's book *Alice in Wonderland* where Alice and the Cheshire Cat met at a fork in the road. Alice said to the Cat, "Would you tell me, please, which way I ought to go from here?"

"That depends a good deal on where you want to get to," said the Cat.

"I don't much care where," said Alice.

"Then it doesn't matter which way you go," purred the Cat.

"So long as I get somewhere," Alice added as an explanation.

"Oh, you're sure to do that," said the Cat, "if you only walk long enough."

The lesson here is that we need to know where we want to go. You don't have to know *exactly* where, but you better at least know the general direction.

The topic of goal setting has received a lot of attention from sport psychologists, coaches, managers, and anyone else who is trying to get you to do more than you are currently doing. The primary teaching one hears from these experts is that (1) you must have goals and (2) they must be specific. Without clear goals, you will fail to succeed.

The next step, they explain, is a process in which you state your goals and write them down. Once you have clearly stated your intended goals, the magic begins, and one day, you will have achieved your goals because you *wrote them down*.

I just don't buy it. Sure goals help, and writing them down helps reinforce them, but the fact of the matter is that people succeed every day without clearly stated goals. That's because these people have something that is even more important—they have *intention*.

Intention is powerful because it addresses the question of *why*. Why are you getting up early to work out? Why are you staying late at work to check up on your employees? You can have intention without a clearly defined goal and accomplish great things, but if you have a goal without intention, you'll usually fall well short of your dreams.

Recently, I met with several of my college fraternity brothers to catch up. A number of these guys have been very successful in business and have made quite a bit of money over the years. One of my friends, Greg Jordan, had recently sold his company to a larger company and had agreed to stay on as a manager for a couple of years during the transition.

As a way to create accountability among the senior managers, his new boss made everyone attend a conference call on Monday mornings where each manager would tell the group what he or she planned to do that week to enhance the business.

My friend Greg, who had already started and sold several companies and had become quite successful in the process, saw this exercise as both unnecessary and elementary. Finally, it was his turn to report to the group.

"Gentlemen," he said, "this week, I am going to do exactly what I have done every week for the past 25 years—go have some fun and make some money." He said nothing more.

Everyone on the call was quiet as tension filled the air. Greg was telling them that you can be successful without having specific goals by possessing a belief in yourself and your ability to make it happen. It's called the *power of expectation*. It's not how most people typically think, but it's how we should if we want to get somewhere worth going.

KEY TAKEAWAY

If you know where you want to go, you will find the way there, and your way will likely be a route you've never taken before. The *what* comes before the *how*, and the *why* should come before the *what*.

The Big Why

Frequently, I begin conversations with clients by asking them a question regarding goals: "What do you want?" Usually, they are unable to answer.

Can *you* answer that question? What do *you* want?

The Dalai Lama says that we all want peace of mind, contentment. I find that interesting because I know quite a few successful people who are not content. They never seem to be totally satisfied, yet they still enjoy their lives. They embrace the challenge and struggle of life. Once one challenge is complete, they go after another, never spending much time basking in the glow of their success.

When you have intention, you don't need a goal. The goal is not about the *what* and the *how* but about the *why*. I call this the Big Why.

If you are setting a goal without understanding the reason for it, then maybe you should reevaluate the goal in general.

My main problem with most goal setting is that we play it way too safe. Most of us find out what we want (a goal) and then lay out the steps necessary to get there. Simple enough, right? Wrong! More often than not, the goals we set are those we are very confident we can reach. Why should that be a bad thing? Because we need to realize that failing to reach the goal is a part of reaching the goal.

Recently, I was speaking to a group of salespeople who were each asked to set a sales goal that they were 100 percent certain they could reach if they put forth a solid effort.

After everyone in the room had completed the task, I then asked them to stay with the same goal but now rewrite it so that they would be only 90 percent certain they could reach the mark. After a few rumblings, they went to work and rewrote their goals.

"Great!" I said. "You're almost there. Now rewrite the goal so that you are only 80 percent sure you will succeed."

The leader of the group shot me a look as though I might be losing my mind, which is very possible. When they had all finished, I asked them to decide how good they really wanted to be.

"For those of you who are satisfied with keeping your job and maybe getting a modest bonus this year, stop here. But as for the rest of you, let's keep going.

"Okay, now rewrite your goal so that you have only a 70 percent chance of success."

After they completed that round, I asked them again if they wanted to stop or keep going. One salesperson in the middle of the room yelled out, "Hell, yes—keep going!"

I walked up to him, took out my wallet, and gave him $20.

"That attitude will make you a lot of money," I said. "What about the rest of you? How do you feel? Anyone getting nervous?"

A few hands went up.

"Perfect!" I said. "This is what you want—a goal that will get your full attention. One that will get your adrenaline flowing and make you feel like you are approaching the edge. We are almost finished. Now rewrite your goal so that you have only a 60 percent chance of success and a 40 percent chance of failure. *That's* your goal."

That's how you do it. When you set goals, you have to go big. Setting a goal that has no chance of failure is a waste of time. It's nothing more than a pep rally.

Practicing What I Preach

This past year, I turned 50, and I wanted to do something big to mark the occasion. I was working with quite a few distance runners at the time, and I decided I would run another marathon for my birthday. We had been talking quite a lot about setting big goals, and I wanted them all to know that I practiced what I preached—or at least attempted to.

A few weeks into the training, I found myself not very excited about running another marathon. I had become friends with Ian Torrence, an experienced runner who has run over 150 ultra-marathons. (Most ultras are 50K and longer, and Ian has run quite a few 100-milers.)

I asked Ian what I would have to do to run an ultra, and he laid out the commitment I would have to make. Right away, I realized that I could run a 50K and maybe a 50-miler. My motivation and excitement immediately increased.

Upon further study, I came to the conclusion that I had a 90 percent chance of completing another marathon, a 60 percent chance of running the 50K (31 miles), and a 40 percent chance of completing a 50-miler.

The weekend before my birthday, I headed out to my favorite running trail, a one-mile loop, and ran 50K. Friends and family joined me, and it was a fun time (and yes, painful). Had I not increased my goal from a marathon to a 50K, I would not have maintained the interest or the motivation to complete the task. So I introduced a greater risk of failure. Suddenly, the challenge had my attention. It made for a true adventure.

KEY TAKEAWAY

Goals that are not frightening are not worth having.

Every now and then, I hear someone talking about a backup plan, a Plan B. The backup plan is what you do if the primary plan, Plan A, doesn't work out. When we create a Plan B, it's not as much a safety net as it is a noose. It's a great way to sabotage yourself. Anyone with a Plan B is not totally committed to the Plan A. They are hedging their bets. People with a Plan B are planning to fail—they just don't know it yet. Kill Plan B or it will kill you.

It is absolutely imperative that once you have a plan, you fully commit to that plan. The Plan B agenda will keep you from totally committing and ultimately hinder your performance. Having just one plan and fully committing to it is the best strategy for success.

6

• ——————————— •

Setting Expectations

The chief danger in life is that you may take too many precautions.

—Alfred Adler

I met Barbara Parker and her husband, Sean, in 2007 while working with Pete Rea and the Zap Elite team in Blowing Rock, North
Carolina.

At the time, Barbara and Sean were two very good college runners
who would later marry after graduating from Florida State University
(FSU). Barbara is from England, and she had received a scholarship
from FSU to run cross-country, the 1,500 meter, the 5,000 meter, and
the steeplechase.

After a successful collegiate career, Barbara ran professionally with
the goal of becoming an Olympian and representing the United King-
dom. In 2008, she made the U.K. team and ran the steeplechase in
Beijing, China. Unfortunately, she failed to advance past the prelimi-
nary round.

Though she did not run very well at her first Olympics, Barbara
achieved her goal of making the Olympic team. Like most first-time

Olympians, her primary goal was to make the team, not win a race or a medal.

Barbara knew she could run faster, and she continued to train with Sean as her coach. In the summer of 2011, she made the World Cross Country Championship team that competed in Daegu, South Korea. This time, Barbara ran fast enough to get past the prelims and into the finals by placing in the top 15. However, once in the finals, she ran poorly.

Upon telling the story to me for the first time, I asked her what her goal was for the World Cross Country Championships.

"Get to the finals," she said.

At this point, I suggested to her that she always reaches her goal in these big events.

"No, I don't," she fired back.

"Well, think about it, Barbara," I said. "Your goal in 2008 was to make the Olympic team. You did. Your goal at the Worlds was to make the finals. You did."

"Yeah, I made the finals, but I ran terribly and got dropped early in the race," she said.

"But you had no intention of doing anything in that race other than finishing it, and you did that—you finished."

"What do you mean?" she questioned.

"You didn't go into the finals with the intention of placing, and you certainly weren't trying to win the damn thing, now were you? You did exactly what you intended to do, nothing more and nothing less."

At that, Barbara looked down, paused a moment, and said, "Yeah, I guess you're right."

"So, let me ask you this: What is your goal for the 2012 Olympics?"

Barbara thought for a moment. "I definitely want to make it to the finals. I know I can do it because I made the finals at the Worlds. I should make it—I'm one of the 15 best in the world."

"Every morning, all 15 women who are going to make the finals in the women's steeplechase get up, put on their running shoes, and head out to train—right?" I asked her.

Barbara nodded her head, yes.

"Probably all 15 of those women expect to make the finals. They all believe they are good enough to make the finals. Would you agree?"

"Sure," she said.

"And how many of those 15 expect to medal? How many are running today with the intention of winning a medal at the 2012 Olympics in the women's steeple?"

"Oh, I don't know," she said. "There are several Africans who probably think they are going to medal, and the Russian."

"So, is it fair to say that every day, some of the women train with the intention of making the team, some train with the expectation of making the finals, some train with the belief that they are going to medal, and a handful train with the goal of winning?"

Barbara said it was.

"So, here we are, eight months away from the Olympics. Let's call it 240 days. You probably have around 200 days of training left, twice a day, for a total of 400 workouts before the Olympics. Who do you think will train hardest? Do you think the women who are training with the hope of making the team will train with the same focus, intensity, and purpose as those who are training to win the gold medal?"

I continued to explain that if she wakes up every day and her whole purpose for living, for existing, for running, is to be the best in the world and to win a gold medal, she has very little in common with someone who would just like to make the team. It's not even close to the same thing.

The runner who expects to win a gold medal has a huge advantage over the rest of the field. Not just at the time of the race but every day and every training session—and there are 400 training sessions before the Olympics!

If Barbara doesn't expect to win, she has already forfeited the race. And so have you. You have given up your chance to find out just how fast you can go. The best way to approach a race is to win! The only way to find out how good you can really be is to be willing to give everything you have in an attempt to win. The desire to win is the same as the desire to do your best, and only those who are trying to win are trying to do their best.

That's why winning is important. It's the path to finding your best.

KEY TAKEAWAY

In order to do your best, you must expect to win.

Risking It All

As physically talented as Barbara is, she had to be willing to risk everything in order to reach her full potential. That risk included setting a big goal that she might fail to reach.

A few months later, we revisited her 2012 goals, and this time I asked her what it would take to get on the podium, to medal. "Is there any possible scenario in which you can imagine yourself medaling?" I asked.

She thought about it for a while and said, "I have good speed. My last 800 is as fast as anyone's in the world. If I can stay with the lead pack during the first 2,000 meters, I could medal."

"Great! That's your new strategy and goal. So let me ask you, *why* are you running?"

"Because I want to get a medal," she said.

"No, you *expect* to get a medal!"

Everyone wants a medal, but only those who *truly believe* they will get a medal have a chance. *Wanting* a medal is a conscious desire.

Expecting to medal is an unconscious belief. There's a big difference between the two. From that day on, we began each session with my asking Barbara again *why* she was still running. A few months in, we had the following discussion:

"Because I'm going to win a medal in London," she would say.

"Do you really believe that, or are you just telling me what I want to hear?"

"You know, it's really interesting," she said. "At first I had to fake it, but now I am coming to believe that it is true."

In just a few short months, we had gone from trying to get into the finals to expecting to win a medal. Barbara noticed that the intensity and outcome of her training sessions had improved, and she would regularly text me with updates.

In order to gauge her progress, Sean would have Barbara repeat certain workouts every few weeks to determine where she needed to improve. Across the board, her attitude toward difficult workouts had changed.

We discussed that if you truly want to get better, then you have to *want* your workouts to be hard, to be painful. It makes no sense to wish away the difficult once you realize that it is essential to your improvement. In order to run a personal best, one must be willing to hurt. If you are wishing away the pain, you are also wishing away the thing that's going to make you better.

One has to learn that pain is the desired state and to not wish it away when it comes.

KEY TAKEAWAY

Expectation dictates performance. Everyone wants
to win, but only a very few expect to win.

In my work with corporate clients, I see the same challenges. Most of us have strong beliefs regarding what we believe is possible at work, and what is impossible. As a general rule, a majority of us underestimate ourselves and thus underestimate what we are capable of doing. In my work with sales teams, it is important that a sales representative realizes that before she goes into a sales meeting, she must have an expectation of what is about to happen. In other words, she must believe that there are *possible* and *impossible* outcomes in a meeting.

Research suggests that about half of sales reps will not make a second call after being told "No" on the first attempt. After a second "No," 75 percent of sales reps view the possibility of doing business with this client as nonexistent and never call again. If the sales rep gets a third "No," then only about 12 percent of the initial population will still be willing to engage the client. Interestingly enough, studies show that most clients say "Yes" after the fourth engagement.

If you are under the impression that once someone tells you "No" once or twice, it means it's impossible to ever do business, than you are going to be at a terrible disadvantage.

Let's look at an example of this in action.

I have a good friend, Greg Fisher, who has been extremely successful in the financial services industry. One day we were talking about a customer whom I had previously worked with, but I had lost the account after they hired a new VP of human resources. Greg knew I was going back to New York City where the client was based and suggested I stop in and visit the CEO. I couldn't understand why he thought that was a good idea, given the fact that the company had not continued my contract. Greg simply said, "Some of my best clients are ones who had fired me in the past but who came to respect the fact that I don't give up easily."

●———●

Winning is never impossible—just look at the sports page of the newspaper. Every day, in every city in America, you can pick up a sports page and read about something that happened the day before that was not supposed to happen.

The best team doesn't always win, even the all-star has a bad night, and the "nobody" can become "somebody." Everyone has a story about the very first time they did something they were never supposed to accomplish. That's the wonder of life—doing the impossible for the first time.

The impossible happens every day in business as well. We just have to understand that these kinds of things don't just happen to other people—they can happen to us as well! But first we must believe that this big crazy miracle called "life" includes each and every one of us.

Remember: Fear is your opponent. No one is better or faster than you—only less afraid.

Barbara's Expectations

In June 2012, after five months of training with a winning attitude, Barbara ran the steeplechase in the Prefontaine Classic in Eugene, Oregon. Five of the top seven women in the world were at the starting line.

Prior to this race, we had been working on Barbara's taking the risk of going out with the lead runners and establishing herself as one of the runners who expect to medal. During our last session before the race, I suggested she think of herself as a candle. At the beginning of the race, you light the candle. Your goal is to burn the candle all the way down until it begins to flicker.

Then, just as you cross the finish line, take the risk of letting the candle burn out.

It's true—most runners don't want to die during a race. But winning a race is about being *willing* to die during the race. The idea is to preserve nothing and sacrifice everything. That is what "flying" is all about. You have to leave the safety of the ground and take the risk of crashing.

KEY TAKEAWAY

If you want to fly, you must be willing to risk crashing.

Several weeks before this conversation, Barbara had run in China, but she was unable to take the ultimate risk and assert herself at the beginning of the race. It was her first steeplechase race of the season, and her confidence was not yet high enough.

Today was different.

It was a strange race from the beginning. For one, the starter's gun wasn't working properly. The women took their places at the line, and the gun misfired—false start. They backed up and waited to take their places at the line again. They lined up.

Another false start.

After the second false start, the television cameras panned from the infield, showing the women—all of whom had stepped back, waiting for the third attempt at a start. That is, everyone except for Barbara, who stood an entire foot in front of the other women.

Though she was not conscious of it, she was already asserting herself. She felt that she deserved to be in front, deserved to be on the track with the world's best runners. Before the race even began, she was standing out in front of everyone else.

Barbara went out with the leaders and stayed in the lead pack of the race for its entirety. The result was a fourth-place finish and a new U.K. record by five seconds, as well as a personal best.

In the weeks following, we met and reviewed the tape of the race. I showed her where she was standing in front of the other women prior to the start. Barbara had no idea that she had been asserting herself before the race had even begun.

That's the power of the unconscious mind: expectation.

7

·————————·

Embracing the Team Mindset

The main ingredient of stardom is the rest of the team.

—John Wooden

don't believe in *individual performance*. Before you get upset, I am quite aware that this is not a popular view in the land of the free and the home of the brave. But regardless, simply stated, no one has ever done anything completely on his or her own.

Of course, there is the illusion of the self-made man: the guy who delivered papers when he was a kid, then advanced to stock boy at the local grocery during high school. Next, he put himself through college by working during the day and going to school at night. After working a couple of years for a larger company, he learned the ropes and developed a wonderful work ethic. Then, he started his own company, and 20 years down the road, he was ultra-successful, and he had big money, a large company, and a massive ego.

When asked about his success, he tells the story of how no one ever gave him a thing and how he worked two jobs to put himself through college. We've all heard this one a hundred times.

But what about the part of the story that never gets told?

What about the people who helped him survive after his birth? What about the great grade-school teacher who cared about him and taught him how to read? What about the neighbor who helped him get the job delivering papers?

The untold story is always the most interesting one.

We all love a good cowboy movie, and we always cheer when the underdog defeats the perennial powerhouse. But the good guys get there only because they had a team helping them every step of the way.

At the end of the day, we all need some help to become great.

KEY TAKEAWAY

No one has ever accomplished anything on his own.
There is no such thing as individual performance.

The Importance of a Supportive Environment

People are successful primarily because they have some innate talent, which they were born with. These same individuals find themselves in an environment in which someone nurtures their talent and encourages them, and then gives them the opportunity to show off what they can do.

Throughout the years, I have held hundreds of sessions with individual collegiate athletes. One after the other, they have told me how they performed very well in high school, but now things were not working out as well in college.

Trends began to emerge, and I soon realized that if I was ever going to help these athletes, I would need to get them all in a room at the same time because they were all experiencing the same thing.

The commonality for these struggling athletes, I found, was that they had a strong supportive environment back home, but they had not been able to re-create this positive environment while at college. They either had failed to create a good relationship with the coach, or they were at odds with one or more of their teammates.

When I got them together in a group, it didn't take much to get them talking. If the team was struggling, I would simply start by asking them why they thought they weren't playing well. After the first person spoke up, the others couldn't wait to get their two cents in.

The teams that were most successful spoke up more easily than the ones that were struggling. I would ask the good teams how good they thought they *could* be.

"Can you all win a conference championship? Can you win *the* national championship?"

Then I would ask them, if they had failed to win a championship, what had stopped them from going all the way? The issues on higher-performing teams were usually more tightly defined and centered around maintaining focus, intensity, and the good fortune needed to go long into the playoffs.

But the lower-performing teams almost always had a serious problem with the coach (or coaching staff), or the teams had become fractured and subteams had been established. Certain players would not speak to one another, and after a poor performance, the blame game would begin.

It was always someone else's fault. The anger and frustration were palpable. At times, it was very stressful just to sit in the room with these underperforming teams. However, once the athletes were able to share their hurt and anger without being destructive to one another, the situation would improve, and performance would rebound.

I learned that the ideal situation for developing the skills of these athletes was to work with them both as individuals *and* as a group. This model was revised for my corporate clients, and as a result, we have developed an outstanding leadership development program.

A sportswriter for the local newspaper at the time had heard that I was working with entire teams, and he called to ask if he could interview me about the work we were doing. During the interview, I shared with him that the concept of a "team"—truly being a unified group—was quite rare in sports, and it happens only when serious intention and discipline are in place.

I explained that athletes are not going to come together as a unit when they don't know the other people on the team or if they don't trust one another. Furthermore, people work together when they are convinced that they can't obtain the goal without their teammates' help.

If a person thinks he or she can make it alone, they will not collaborate with others.

The Process of Team Building

The process of building a team has several critical components. One or more is usually missing, and thus the team never jells, and it fails to perform at its full potential. Below are the six steps I have found to be critical to teamwork.

Step 1. Recruit and Select the Right People

The first step to having a great team is selecting people who are individually talented and who also have the maturity and desire to be a part of something much bigger than themselves. These people have to want to be a member of the team and be willing to adopt the culture and values of the team.

This is the primary role of the coach in sports or the manager in business. The leader must have an eye for talent and be able to differentiate between candidates. If leadership fails during the selection process, there will never be a chance for success.

Recently, I was in Dallas, Texas, with a group of VP-level managers who were participating in an experiential leadership program. On this particular day, we visited St. Philips Academy, a private school in one of the worst parts of Dallas.

Crack houses were once located where the school now exists. The director of the school, Dr. Terry Flowers, spoke to our group about his leadership style and how he has been able to defy the odds and create a school that has a 100 percent high school graduation rate in an area where this was once viewed as impossible.

I asked Dr. Flowers what his role was in the selection process for new hires. He quickly responded that he interviews everyone who comes to work in the school. On only very few occasions, when he had been out of town, had someone been hired without first getting his approval. He added that he generally knows within the first 10 minutes if a person will fit into his culture.

I then asked him what he was looking for in a candidate. Without hesitation, he explained that the person must love children in order to join his staff: "If you don't love children, you can't teach them." That is his primary objective, to find teachers and staff who love children. After that, the teaching happens automatically.

Step 2. Develop Strong Friendships

Once you pick your team, individuals must come to know one another in a fairly intimate way, and this is typically done through the sharing of their life stories.

It is imperative that they know about each other's pain and disappointments because they must show vulnerability and take the risk of being rejected for who they truly are. If teammates share only their successes and achievements, trust will never develop. There is no trust without risk and vulnerability.

One exercise that I like to do with teams who are trying to strengthen their bond is to ask each of them whom they consider to be their best friend on the team and why. I also ask them whom they don't feel close to and why. For the kids who don't have friends on the team, the reason is typically because they have not spent much time together or they believe they don't have much in common.

Another exercise that I find helpful is having the athletes share their family stories, including specific information on their parents and siblings. And the final exercise involves each athlete's sharing the best and worst days of his or her life. This exercise is usually followed by surprise and tears.

Step 3. Create a Shared Belief System

Everyone must agree on the absolutes of the team—the team rules or mission. This includes what can never happen and what must happen on a regular basis.

On successful teams, there is usually a motto or some unifying belief that everyone holds to be true. There is a priority—a first and most important thing.

When I worked with Tubby Smith and the men's basketball team at the University of Georgia, they would huddle up, put their hands together in the middle, and shout "Hard work." Tubby believed that getting maximum effort was critical to the team's success. Shauna Estes-Taylor and the women's golf team at the University of Arkansas had the motto "Do the possible." They believed it was important to focus on what you can do and hit shots you are 100 percent sure you can execute.

When it comes to a team, the primary rule should be that members are expected to make and keep their promises. Breaking a promise is a serious offense, and excuses are not tolerated. One of the most common team promises I hear is, "Do what you say you are going to do." Whether that means showing up on time or telling others they can count on you, you must be sure to deliver. Truth telling and promise keeping are critical, and these ideas must be introduced early in the season, before you start competing.

Athletes learn very early in the season which players they will be able to count on when times get hard and the game is on the line. Believing in each other is actually an aggregate of many small things a person says or does over the course of days, weeks, and months. Showing up late for a meeting or not doing schoolwork or similar tasks says a lot about who can be counted on when you need them the most.

The same should be true for professional organizations, but it sadly seems to not be the case in today's world.

In most of the organizations I consult with, the competition is not another company who provides the same product or service. Instead, the competition comes from *inside* the organization. People who are supposed to be colleagues working for the same outcome are actually plotting strategically against their own team members. They are competing for attention, money, and promotions. They think about how others are doing and how they need to position themselves in order to look better than the other people on the team.

When organizations don't work together (and most don't), they compete against one another. This is a waste of time, energy, and ultimately financial resources, and it is painful to watch.

Most companies tell their employees, "We want you to work together as a team" because they understand that group production goes up when we collaborate and encourage one another. The problem arises when companies reward their employees for acting independently and selfishly, not collaboratively. Most organizations still believe in the impact of the talented individual. They put more time and money into finding and hiring talented individuals than they put into getting a group of people to work effectively together. This is very obvious in professional sports. The majority of the conversation is about the production of a specific individual, not the impact the athlete has on his or her teammates.

In the end, most people are going to keep doing the actions that the company rewards, not the actions the company has written down on a mission statement.

Step 4. Fight Without Hurting Each Other

Conflict is inevitable, and the avoidance of conflict only creates more conflict. Teams that try to "play nice" are usually not very successful. Members must learn to fight and manage conflict without its becoming destructive—and you can do this by making truthfulness the primary intention when communicating.

Anyone can be truthful without being mean or hurtful. Sure, honesty can make others feel uncomfortable, but that is not the intention, and intention is critical in communication and relationship building. Knowing that you are being honest in order to improve your relationship with a teammate is far more effective than being honest just to make someone else feel bad.

Let's look at some real-life examples of intention in action.

When I work with men's teams, I ask the men to talk about how they fought with their brothers growing up—and their intentions when they fought. What I've heard most often is that while it's okay to cause your brother pain, it is not okay to have the intention to *injure* him. Injury does damage to the person. Pain does not and is usually temporary.

When I work with women's teams, we talk about how they fought with their sisters. What I've heard in these conversations is similar to what I've heard from men's teams: If you hurt her feelings, you have to apologize afterward.

What do these examples prove?

That you can tell the truth and fight with someone in a way that harms and in a way that doesn't—but the end result is all about your intention.

Step 5. Cultivate Strong Leaders

A successful team must have someone who they look to for leadership. Yes, the coach must be an effective leader, but there must also be leadership among the athletes. Coaches who are unable to groom leaders from within their teams will never be successful.

Unfortunately, most organizations, whether in sports or business, do not have effective leadership. There are people in leadership roles, but they are not actually leading or inspiring others to reach their full potential. Instead, they tend to just boss their subordinates around.

In my observations, the worst leaders are typically the most senior people in an organization. Usually the best leaders come from two or more levels of management beneath the CEO. Why? Because senior leaders are often out of touch. They don't know their people, and their people don't know them. Because of their position, they make the mistake of assuming they are the best leaders in their organizations when this may not actually be the case.

Step 6. Clearly Define the Team Goal

Success is clearly defined by a single *team* goal. No individual agendas can be tolerated. The self must be sacrificed in order for the team to excel.

It amazes me how frequently coaches emphasize the success of the team all year long and then have an awards banquet at the end of the year and spend two hours handing out individual trophies like MVP and Most Improved. They believe it encourages and promotes future success, when in reality it does neither.

Business leaders make the same mistake. They too profess the benefits of working as a team and achieving group goals, and then they hand out Employee of the Month awards.

The best kinds of leaders create a culture with goals and awards that either everyone or no one achieves. Once you create an environment where there are winners and losers at the same time, you will never truly have a team. Everyone must win or no one wins. No exceptions.

●————●

Twenty years ago, American culture valued the name on the front of the jersey more than the name on the back. In fact, there was a time when there was no name on the back of the jersey.

In 1929, the Yankees were the first team to make numbers a permanent part of the baseball uniform. Numbers were handed out in the order of the lineup (Babe Ruth was no. 3 because he batted third, Lou Gehrig no. 4 because he batted fourth, and so on). The individual was seen primarily as a member of the team. He was valuable only to the extent that he could help his team win.

In the 1960s and 1970s, there was a collective shift in thinking in our society. What used to be a society of "we" became a society of "me." The self-esteem movement began celebrating the individual. It quit being about how much you contributed to the team, and the focus shifted to individual egos and personalities instead. Recently, I heard a senior member of the NBA state that the NBA was a "league of personalities." He also believed the league should promote the players, not the teams. It's sad to me that most fans come to watch a particular player, not a team.

Today, we value the name on the back of the jersey more than the name on the front, and it comes at a high price to the goals of the team. In 2012, the NBA estimated it would make in excess of $100 million in jersey sales that year, while 22 of the 30 teams were losing money. What does that statistic tell you? If you were told that there was a business in which 73 percent of the franchise owners lost money, would you invest?

How is this business model possible? Because today the NBA promotes individual players instead of the team.

Fifty years ago, fans pulled for a *team*. If a player left that team, the kid no longer rooted for that player. Today, that is rare. Instead, kids have favorite players, despite the team they play for. Doing this destroys the value of a team and creates what we have now—a hero worship culture. Players draw attention to themselves, and they celebrate their own personal accomplishments more than the team's victory.

When the focus is on the individual, athletes and employees cease to play as a team. You simply can't claim the team is most important **and** then create incentives that suggest the individuals are more valuable than their teams.

In order to be successful, there must be a unified goal. We all win—or lose—together. And the more we win, the harder we work for each other.

PART II

How the Mind Fails Us

8

Failure Drives Success

You have enemies? Good. That means you've stood up for something.

—Winston Churchill

When I first began my career as a sport psychologist, I needed to make a little extra money to support my wife and two children. A small, private liberal arts college with its main campus some 50 miles from Athens decided to open a satellite campus just a few miles away, so I took the opportunity to teach an introductory psychology class there to make a few extra bucks.

After 10 years of college and three degrees, I thought I should be able to create an interesting and educational learning experience for my students. But it turned out to be much harder than I had thought.

I had never been a fan of teachers who tried to trick or outsmart their students, so I took a very direct and straightforward approach to teaching. I lectured on material from the textbook Monday through Thursday, and I had reviews and weekly tests every Friday. Every question on the test was included in both one of the lectures that week and in the review that I gave the day of the lecture. On Fridays, as soon as the last student finished his or her test, the students graded their own exams. They knew how they had done immediately. I did this for two reasons: first, research has demonstrated that immediate feedback enhances learning, and second, I hated grading papers.

The only other graded part of the course was a 10-page research review paper. Students picked their own topics regarding psychology, and they were allowed to study anything that was of interest to them.

On the first day, I reviewed the syllabus with the class. It clearly stated that papers were due at the beginning of class on their due date. The instructions also stated that late papers would not be accepted and that students would receive a grade of zero if their papers were late for any reason.

I explained to the class that part of my job was to prepare them for the real world. One day, they would all (hopefully) have a job and a boss who gave them assignments with a deadline. If they failed to meet the deadline, there would be consequences, including the possibility of being fired.

I wanted them to understand that I was being inflexible not because I wanted to be mean but because I wanted them to be prepared for life after college. At the end, I told them it was likely that at least one of them would fail to meet the deadline and would be enraged when I would not make an exception.

Sure enough, on the day the papers were due, one young man failed to appear at the beginning of class. With several minutes remaining, he showed up and took his seat. After class, he approached me and stated that he had completed the paper with plenty of time remaining, but his printer was not working, so he had to drive to a copy center to have his paper printed. He handed me his work and said again how sorry he was that it was late.

"Me too," I said. "This paper is 30 percent of your grade, and unfortunately, you will receive no points for the paper."

He couldn't believe that I wouldn't accept his paper, and he continued to explain why it was really not a big deal and how it would be okay with him if I wanted to deduct some points for the paper being late.

His protest fell on deaf ears. I suggested that he take his case to the dean of the department.

The following day, the dean asked me to stop by his office before class. I did as requested, and he very politely told me why my decision was not a good one and how it would be in everyone's best interest if I would accept the student's paper.

I held my ground and suggested that we were actually doing the student a favor by helping him learn the importance of a deadline and the value of planning ahead. After several more minutes of discussion, we remained at a stalemate.

I suggested to the dean that if he did not like my decision, he could simply override it by changing the grade I gave the student after I turned in my grades for the quarter. He asked me to grade the paper anyway and submit it to him with my final grades.

I gave the kid an 80 on his paper. It was actually pretty good. But I gave him a zero in the grade book.

I later learned that the dean had taken my grade of 80, subtracted 10 points for tardiness, and had given the student credit for the paper. The following semester, I was asked to come back to the school to teach another course. The dean told me that my teacher evaluation scores were very good and that the kids really liked me. I declined. What's the use of being a teacher if you can't teach what really matters most?

Demanding the best from people, holding them accountable, not accepting their excuses, and telling them to do something again are not acts of brutality—they are acts of love. If you truly care about people, you will run the risk of their becoming angry with you when you do not acquiesce when things get hard.

The best managers and coaches challenge their people. They push them to their limits, and they create stressful situations so that when difficult times appear, they will be prepared.

There is no success without failure. Success is what you do after you fail. The people in my life who have become great successes have also suffered through quite a few failures. Those who avoid failure or try to help others avoid failure are really just impeding their progress.

I believe we failed in our responsibility when it came to the student who did not turn in his paper on time. Why? Because we did not allow him to fail and learn from his experience. I imagine he went into the workforce and failed to meet other deadlines because he never learned from the pain of failure the first time.

I have a good friend who has been a college professor for many years. He recently told me that parents frequently call him to discuss their child's grade in his class. He stated that when he first started teaching, he never received phone calls from parents. Yet now, it's a regular occurrence, and the parent usually requests that he make a special exception for their child. After all, that's what they have done throughout the child's entire life.

Failure itself is not a bad thing, but repeating the same mistake over and over is a tragedy. There is rarely a time in life when one cannot recover from failure. However, having consecutive failures can be unrecoverable. One of the reasons people have consecutive failures is that they are unable to see the value of or learn from the lesson of the first failed attempt.

Golf is a great example of this truth. Professional golfers will play a poor shot, but they almost always use the poor shot to help them refocus and become more intentional in their next shot. Therefore, they rarely hit two bad shots in a row.

Amateur golfers, on the other hand, tend to respond differently to a poor shot. They become angry and lose their ability to focus on the task at hand, and they are more likely to hit consecutive poor shots—a mistake from which it is almost impossible to recover.

One of the best stories that demonstrate the interconnected relationship of success and failure involves one of the best athletes in history. Michael Jordan was a tenth grader at Laney High School in Wilmington, North Carolina, when he failed to make the varsity basketball team.

The story goes that Michael was only 5 feet, 11 inches at the time, and he was not yet good enough to play at the varsity level. To make matters worse, one of his tenth-grade friends—who was taller and better—did make the varsity team. This failure was so humiliating to Michael that he worked hard to make sure it never happened again.

It was during this time that Michael developed one of the best-known work ethics in all of sports. He was able to take this experience of failure and use it to propel him for years to come. In Michael's own words, "It all started when Coach Herring cut me. What it did was instill some values in me. It was a lesson to me to dig within myself."

One can't help but wonder what would have happened if the coach had decided not to cut Michael Jordan from the team and let him move up with his friend. There would be no harm in showing a kid some mercy, right? Experiencing success instead of failure could very well have been a curse to Michael, and we may have never seen the greatest basketball player of all time had he made varsity in his tenth-grade year.

To prove my point, you know the name of the tenth grader who made the team instead of Michael Jordan? His name is Harvest Leroy Smith.

Michael was so appreciative of the lesson he learned from Smith and Coach Herring that he would frequently check into hotels with the alias "Leroy Smith" so as not to alert others that he was in town.

Don't feel too bad for Mr. Smith though. Even though he is not widely known, he did attend the University of North Carolina, Charlotte, on a basketball scholarship, and he played some pro ball overseas. Smith later became a successful businessman, and he will always enjoy the satisfaction of knowing he played a key role in the development of one of the greatest athletes of our time.

The common belief is that you become successful by avoiding failure. But this is not true because successful people fail! Everyone fails. Instead, success is defined by your response to failure.

When things are not going your way, these challenges or "failures" in life have the capacity to be very informative. They help us create a better awareness of ourselves.

Not only can you not avoid failure, but you *need* failure to get better. When you fail and you will run into it and learn the lesson right away.

9

•————————•

The Curse of Perfection

Do what you can with what you have, where you are.

—Teddy Roosevelt

Most elite athletes—from golfers to gymnasts, placekickers, and baseball pitchers—tend to be very focused, disciplined, and perfectionistic. Their belief is that the desire to be "perfect" will end up making them better. Unfortunately, this is not always true. More often than not, the desire to be perfect actually *hinders* performance. When we try to be perfect, we assume that success equals not making any mistakes, when in fact, success is your *response to the mistake*. People who tend to be perfectionists do not respond well to adversity or defeat. Their belief is "If I'm doing it correctly, there will be no struggle or failure." As we mentioned in the previous chapter, loss and pain are the great motivators to change. Well, defeat, struggle, and embarrassment can also be added to that list because they can all lead to change as well. And remember, change always leads to improvement.

Not understanding that failure is part of the journey of success will lead to *more* failure—not perfection. Perhaps the best and easiest way to define success is this: Fall down 100 times, get up 101.

Accepting the Good and the Bad

We must accept that every now and then, we will have a bad day. When I talk with elite athletes, I ask them the following question: "If you were the best athlete in the world in your event, how frequently would you have a bad day?" Surprisingly, many great athletes believe they should get to a point where they no longer have any bad days (or failures). But in reality, the best and most self-aware of those athletes report that during the course of a 30-day month, they have somewhere between 3 and 6 bad days. They understand that having a bad day is simply part of the process. The ability to accept these fluctuations in performance allows athletes to remain fully engaged in their training and keep their goals high. Likewise, the inability to make sense of your failures will ultimately cause you to become discouraged and less motivated, and your performance will decline as a result.

How you function during a good day does not define your character. It's how you function during a bad day that is the true test. It is always beneficial for me to see an athlete I am working with have a bad day because it is the truest measure of that person's competitive ability. Do they exacerbate the bad day by becoming even more critical of themselves or someone else? Do they feel sorry for themselves and pout? Do they make excuses and quit? In order for you to reach your potential, you must know how you respond to poor performance. This is critical information you simply cannot move forward without.

If perfect is not the goal, what is? It's simple: *Do your best.* That's it. Each and every day, make it your intention to do the very best you can with what you have that day. As I said earlier, in your daily journal, give yourself a W or an L for each day. If you did the best you could that day, you get a W. If you did not do your best, you get an L. The goal is to have six or fewer Ls in a month. And you never want to have two consecutive Ls. It's okay to have a bad day, but you must make yourself recover quickly and get back on track. Remember: The goal is not to be perfect. It's to do your best and recover quickly from failure.

What Is Perfection?

Perfection is a mathematical concept, not a human one. Those who actually achieve perfection, or the human equivalent of perfection, probably aren't trying to be perfect when they actually bump into the "perfect" moment.

Gymnasts and distance runners have much in common psychologically because they both tend to be obsessive and have desires to be perfect. During one practice with a top college gymnastics team in the 1990s, I shared with the young women the story of Nadia Comaneci's "perfect" 10.0 during the 1976 Olympics. Nadia, a member of the Romanian team, won three gold medals during the 1976 Olympics in Montreal, and she scored the first perfect 10.0. At age 14, she scored a 10.0 on her uneven bars routine. Because it was believed to be impossible to score a perfect 10.0 at that time, the scoreboard could display no score higher than a 9.9. In order to present her score, the officials had to present it as a 1.0. At first the crowd was confused, but they soon figured out that she had in fact scored a perfect 10.0. Nadia went on to score six more perfect 10.0s during her Olympic career.

Most of the gymnasts I was working with were familiar with the story, but they were either not born yet or were infants during the 1976 Olympics. In their time, perfect 10.0s were quite common in college gymnastics, and most of the women on the team had been recipients of a 10.0 at some point in their career. One of the women on the University of Georgia (UGA) team, Karen Lichey, was regarded as one of the best gymnasts in college at the time and still remains one of the best ever.

The purpose of presenting the Nadia Comaneci story was to address two concepts at once: *perfection* and *impossible*. I shared my thoughts that in the past, "perfection" had been paired with "impossible," but now perfection (scoring a 10.0) is commonly viewed as possible in college gymnastics. "What's the next impossible thing that will become possible?" I asked the team. We discussed how 200 was the highest possible team score and that no team had ever scored a 200. Additionally, no individual had ever scored a 40 (a perfect 10 on all four events) during a collegiate gymnastics meet. Most of the women believed that someone would eventually score a 40, and several of them had gotten close already. Later that year, Karen Lichey did the impossible and scored a perfect 40 during a meet. When she and I discussed it during our next session, she shared with me that she had come to realize that a 40 was possible and that she had the ability to pull it off. Karen also shared with me a quote by Walt Disney that our mutual friend, Kirk Smith, had given her before the meet. The Disney quote read: "It's kind of fun to do the impossible."

Sixteen years have passed since Karen Lichey scored the first perfect 40 in women's college gymnastics, and at the time of this book's publication, no one else has matched her accomplishment. Many have certainly tried, but with no luck. The best advice you could give a gymnast trying to score the next 40 would be, "Don't try to be perfect. Just perform the routine to the best of your ability. Let the judges worry about the score."

●————●

Many years ago, I had a client who was an artist. She was a very talented young woman who was quite a poet and a painter, but she was frustrated because she was having a block and unable to produce anything that she felt was of value.

In discussing her problem, we realized that the main thing holding her back was her belief that everything had to be perfect in order for her to do her best work. Her stars were not lining up the way she had hoped.

I asked about her belief that everything had to be perfect in order for her to sit down and write. She had assumed that a perfect outcome first required a perfect situation. I suggested that she give up on perfect and just work with what she had.

She agreed to write at a certain time each day, no matter what, to see what would happen. Here is what she brought back to our next session:

> *Don't wait for an invitation, an ideal time, a perfect situation.*
> *It's happening all around you, about you, with or without you.*
> *So, do the do that makes you, you.*
> *Don't wait for another time when you have one available . . . now.*

10

What Does *Focus* Really Mean?

The only thing worse than being blind is having sight but no vision.

—HELEN KELLER

The word *focus* gets used way too often, and most people who tell someone to focus don't truly understand what they are suggesting.

You can go to any Little League park in the country, and in a matter of minutes, some adult will yell, "Come on, you guys, you gotta focus!" The kids have no idea what the grown-ups are saying, and neither do the grown-ups.

In business, we frequently hear of poor performers described as lacking or having no focus. We hear statements like, "This guy is all over the place. He has no focus."

●————●

Focus is actually a visual concept. It has to do with what you are or should be looking at. It is also present tense—it's a *now* concept. Where your eyes are focused is critical to your performance.

In business and in life, focus is more about the image one holds in the brain—the mind's eye, if you will. Many spiritual or meditative practices require the person to focus or look at an image or icon for an extended period of time. This leads to a change in the internal state, or at least that is the intention.

Likewise, looking at a beautiful image or piece of artwork is an act of focus with specific intention. The magic is that as you look at something, what you see changes. Though the object doesn't change, what you see does. As you sustain your focus on something, what you are able to see expands and becomes more intricate.

Trained observers see things that untrained observers cannot see. This is quite amazing when you think about it—two people looking at the same thing and seeing two different things, or one not seeing anything at all.

A perfect example of this phenomenon is the ability of an expert in a given field. Let's say, for example, that you are a fairly good golfer with a 12 handicap and you want to get down into the single digits. Your local pro is a great guy, but he's taken you as far as he can. Knowing that you are still unsatisfied with your game, he suggests you go see one of the teachers that several touring pros in the area work with. You pack your clubs and head out to see the great golf guru.

Upon arrival, you are asked to warm up because he wants to see you hit some balls. Before you begin to hit, he sets up five cameras: one in front, one in back, one to your right, one to your left, and one overhead. Every angle is covered. You hit a few balls with a number of different clubs, and in a short while the expert says, "That's enough. Let's go look at the tape."

The pro shows you the tape in real-time speed, and he comments that you are breaking your wrist at the top of your swing. When you look at the tape in real-time speed, you can't see what the pro sees. He knows this, so he slows the tape down and, sure enough, there it is. At the top of your swing, your wrist breaks, and your club head drops, causing a flaw in your swing. He shows you the problem from several other angles until you are convinced that you too can see what he sees.

After the video analysis, you are wondering why no one else noticed the problem. The guys you play with are all really good, and your pro back home is a scratch golfer. Why didn't anyone pick up on this? The fact of the matter is that they were looking but didn't *see*. You have to train your eye to see by knowing what and how to focus.

What to Look At

Seeing does you no good if you don't know what to look at. Once the golfer has mastered his swing, the focus should then remain external. By "external," I mean the golfer should then train himself on what to look at.

When I work with golfers, I have them stand on the tee with a driver in hand and look for a directional target. This is usually a tree or some object way off in the distance that the golfer will aim toward. After identifying the target, I ask them to visualize the trajectory of the ball going toward the target. It is imperative that golfers be able to see the flight of the ball *before* attempting to execute the shot. If you can't imagine it, then you're probably not going to be able to do it. This process of using a directional target is true for all shots that require a full swing.

At some point, depending on the golfer's ability, the aim goes from hitting the ball *toward* the hole to hitting the ball *into* the hole. Focus and target must change in order for this to happen. Once they are about 100 yards away from the hole and can see the green and flagstick, I ask this question: "Where would the ball need to land in order to go into the hole?"

Surprisingly, most have not thought about holing out from 100 to 125 yards. But the focus or target changes once you begin trying to hit the ball *into* the hole. Specifically, golfers need to find a spot on the turf that they want to hit with the understanding that if the ball hits that spot, it will go into the hole.

Make no mistake, I am not encouraging the golfer to hit it *near* that spot. I want and expect them to hit *the spot*. If they don't think it's possible, they simply will not be able to do it. Most good golfers are surprised that once they are focused on the spot, they begin to hit the ball very close to it and eventually hit the spot.

It's a wonderful thing to observe someone doing something they never thought was possible. After the golfer experiences the magic of focusing on a specific target that is the size of a golf ball, their game is forever changed.

Practicing Focus

Focus takes practice. People usually understand it, but no one actually teaches it. I often do an exercise with athletes to have them think of focus as the beam of a flashlight. You can adjust it to be very large, or you can make it zero in on a particular object. The wide beam is consciousness, while the direct beam is the object of their consciousness. They have to stay tuned in on what that object is. Pretty quickly, they readjust their focus.

After you have learned what to focus on with your eyes, you must then know what to focus on with your brain. In golf, they call this a *swing thought*.

There is a lot of debate about swing thoughts or, for that matter, any conscious thinking in sport. One could easily argue that the best-case scenario is to have a quiet mind that does not think and has no awareness of itself. I agree, but there is only a small percentage of people who can discipline their minds to that level.

Our ability to focus on one particular goal or target is critical for success in both sport and business. One's ability to focus the mind will in turn generate a physical focus or tempo. Tempo is impacted by the mind, and in a situation in which you have a fast and anxious mind, it will lead to a quick or rushed tempo.

Tempo or timing is of great importance in life and in sport. Everyone has a tempo that allows them to be the most relaxed and natural, thus producing the best result.

You can observe the same phenomenon in business. When people get anxious, they talk faster and may begin to twitch or move about in an awkward way.

A perfect metronome for creating consistent timing is our own breath. Our first act of life is to take a breath in, while our last act of life is to let a breath out. Another tool to focus is a breathing exercise I often use with athletes. I ask them to close their eyes and breathe in while saying the word *in*, then breathe out while saying the word *out*. Taking the time to focus on this one simple act allows them to translate it to other aspects of their lives and sport by creating a steady pace.

Pace is critical, and proper focus leads to a steady pace. I often suggest to my clients that they develop a mental approach that will help them stay consistent internally. Continuing with the golf example, I would rather have a golfer count to herself during the swing than say "slow" or "relax." Instead, she should begin her swing with "one," halfway into her backswing is "two," the top of the swing is "three," initiating the downswing is "four," and contact is "five." It is perfectly fine to alter this cadence, but something similar will work for most golfers. After doing this a few hundred times, the mind unconsciously is set to this tempo and will repeat it automatically. If the athlete gets rattled and loses her tempo, she simply goes back to saying it out loud to herself until she is comfortable with her tempo again.

Focus on your target and then on your intention. A big part of success training involves truly understanding *why* you are doing what you are doing, *how* to do it, and *what* it is you are doing. Focus plays a critical role in this process.

11

———●———●———

The Myth of 110 Percent

There are three musts that hold us back: I must do well.
You must treat me well. And the world must be easy.

—Albert Ellis

There is no such thing as 110 percent effort. Even 100 percent is extremely rare. But 90 percent? That will guarantee tremendous success.

Most of us love to brag and let the world know just how hard we are working.

The athlete tells us he's giving it 110 percent, and the businessman informs us that he works 80 hours a week. We're supposed to be impressed, but I'm not. I feel sorry for them. Although effort is important, it isn't the *most important thing*.

Your performance results are what is ultimately recorded, and those results become the metric that you will be measured by. You don't get any extra points for grunting and groaning and making it hard.

While there is a correlation between effort and performance, that correlation is not always positive. Working too hard or putting forth too much effort can actually *decrease* performance. I know of many overtrained athletes and overworked managers who fail to perform well because they are simply exhausted. Their effort is high, but their performance is low. That's why the 110 percent statement is really nothing to brag about.

It is imperative that each person finds his or her ideal effort level—the level that leads to optimal performance. I can't tell you what yours is, but I guarantee you it's not 110 percent.

When we talk about performing at a high level, there are three considerations:

1. The effort or energy exerted
2. The condition of the physical body (Are you tired or injured, for example?)
3. Your mental state (Are you calm, focused, agitated, or upset?)

Together, these three components determine performance.

The Problem with 110 Percent

In our culture, we focus on giving 110 percent effort, but that's more than you actually have. What's interesting is that when you talk to people who have performed at a very high level, they often say it felt easy and at times effortless. They weren't thinking about trying harder or putting forth more effort—their mind was quiet and focused on one thing. They were, as we say, "in the zone." Yes, they were trying, but they were not fighting against themselves and making themselves perform—it naturally happened or it didn't.

Often, when your effort level is at 80 to 90 percent, your body is at 90 percent, and your mind is quiet—you may even feel it's at zero. That's what leads to a high performance.

Here's why.

In competition, you are already putting forth a greater effort because the sympathetic nervous system is aroused. Adrenaline is now in your blood, and your body is working harder, putting forth more effort without your consciously trying harder. It's a wonderful thing, but not when you add even more effort to the equation.

The better mental strategy for a competitive environment is to remain relaxed by putting forth a moderate to high effort in the beginning and then increasing your effort if you need to. Research has shown that successful people are both conscientious and possess a moderate level of anxiety about their performance. If you are already successful and trying to get to the next level, adding more effort or stress will not likely be of much help.

Whether you like it or not, you are an expert at self-deception. We all are.

Most people lie about their level of effort and performance, and their superiors unfortunately play along with the lie in an attempt to be nice. All you've got is 100 percent—it's your absolute best effort, and it's all you are capable of. But rarely do human beings invest 100 percent of themselves into any activity, and rarely is their performance optimal if they do.

My estimate is that when most people are really trying, they are giving an effort of between 70 and 80 percent. Because of this, we have come to believe that 80 percent is our full exertion. On the rare occasion that someone really exerts himself for an extended period of time and moves the needle up to, say, 90 percent, he has the sensation of realizing his best, and that's when you might hear him say, "I gave it 110 percent."

But he didn't. *All anyone has* is 100 percent, and most great athletes and successful businesspeople hit the 100 percent mark only once every few weeks. If you can sustain an 80 percent level of effort on a regular basis, you will be extremely successful.

The Law of Least Effort

This past year I began working with the University of Arkansas men's track and field team. Chris Bucknam is the head coach of the team and one of the best coaches in the country. He has a witty sense of humor and an infectious laugh. However, he does not suffer fools and clearly speaks his mind.

I think he initially had some doubts about some of my ideas, especially the Law of Least Effort. This law basically states that you can get a high level of production without exerting a high level of effort. One thing I had noticed working with both runners and swimmers is that they go the fastest when they don't exert a maximum effort. We talked a lot about the idea of helping athletes find the optimal level of effort in order to perform their best. After discussing this idea, I returned to campus several months later to work with the team. During that visit, Chris shared with me that 87 seems to be the magic number. He said that when he tells an athlete to exert 87 percent of his effort, he finds that tends to lead to the best performance.

A true "100 percent performance" is not just a complete physical effort. In order for us to maximize our abilities, we must also be in an optimal *mental* state.

What is remarkable about this condition is that the individual does not have an experience of trying hard or fully exerting themselves. In fact, the person may have the sensation of effortlessness while performing at this high level.

Resistance

Many times, effort is about resistance. I believe we are truly at our best when we accept what is and work with it versus trying to change or stop it. Exerting force against something is quite different than working with it.

Think of paddling a canoe in a river. You can go with the current or against it. The greatest of us figure out how to go *with* the current, while the rest fight the current and then brag about their 110 percent effort.

When we talk about someone's being in the "zone" or "flow"—that is, in the mental state associated with the highest level of performance—we are talking about someone who is not resisting the forces around him or her but instead working in concert with them.

Years ago, I was in Pittsburgh for a head injury conference, and the Pittsburgh Penguins were in town playing hockey. I decided to head down to the arena and was fortunate enough to get a seat quite close to the action.

Mario Lemieux was playing that night, and the fans were excited. Lemieux had had serious health problems throughout his career, which had limited his playing time. The previous year, he had to sit out with an uncertain future and had retired the following year, in 1997, only to come out of retirement and play again.

What I observed that night was something I have witnessed only a few times in my life. When Lemieux took possession of the puck, time slowed down. He moved in a way that no one else could. Even though he appeared to be in slow motion, he was not. He was in perfect alignment with the external forces around him. He was going downstream while everyone else seemed to be paddling frantically upstream. It appeared effortless.

This is the thing of legends. When we see them, we instantly know that something about them makes them different. Now we know why.

The Problem with Perfect

Many of my clients struggle because they are attempting to do a task perfectly. They believe that "perfect" is the only route to success when in fact, attempting to be perfect is a guarantee that you will not perform to your ability.

When I work with people who are struggling and performing at a level that is lower than their normal ability, I usually advise them to *lower* their effort when doing the task. I also suggest that they intentionally make a mistake. When they stop trying to be perfect, the conscious mind relaxes and allows the natural ability to surface, and an increase in performance is usually the response.

For most people, realizing that less is more comes as a big surprise. They just can't believe it to be true because it is so contrary to what most of us have been taught our entire lives. Instead of focusing on percentages—which are subjective and largely a result of rhetoric and drama—just focus on doing your best.

At the end of each day, ask yourself this question: "Was that the best I could do?"

If you are honest, you will discover that you can rarely answer yes to that question. You'll also realize that the best you can do on Monday may be very different from the best you can do on Tuesday. After all, we are humans—not machines. And with this awareness, you will witness significant differences in your effort level and performance over time.

There will be days when the best you can do is get out of bed and get dressed. There will also be days when you could not make a mistake if you tried. Your stars are aligned, and everything is coming to you with minimal effort. *Long-term success is learning how to acknowledge those differences and not struggle too much on a bad day.*

A bad day is only a day, not a life.

KEY TAKEAWAY

No matter who you are or how successful you have
become, you will have another bad day. Accept it and move on.

After you have shifted your focus from perfect to best, ask yourself: "Did I get better today? Did I move another step toward my goal, my full potential?"

You should be able to answer yes to that question the majority of your days. Once you focus your attention on getting better each day, begin keeping a written record of your performance. On the days you improved, give yourself a W for a win. Days that you fail to advance, give yourself an L for a loss.

Once you are able to get Ws about 80 to 90 percent of the time, you are well on your way to doing something great. Remember: You are not trying to be *the* winner. You are trying to be *a* winner. The greatest men and women are not competing against you. They are competing against themselves each and every day. *You* are your greatest competition. And the next time you hear people brag about how they gave 110 percent, let that be a reminder of what *not* to do or say.

12

●————————————●

The Truth About Winning

Winning isn't getting ahead of others. It's getting ahead of yourself.

—Roger Staubach

There are two primary drives to win. One is healthy, and the other is destructive.

Most people want to win so that they can feel better about themselves. If they can associate themselves and their ego with winning, they come to the conclusion that maybe they are okay after all. And, of course, if they lose, they feel badly because they then come to the conclusion that something is wrong or broken within them.

This state describes the vast majority of us. The emotional responses to both winning and losing are quite obvious, yet most of us have a stronger response to losing (sadness, frustration, anger) than we do to winning (joy, relief, humbled). The competition is an attempt to validate ourselves, to gain approval or recognition from both ourselves and others. We want to win so that we can be "okay."

However, there is a small minority of people who wish to win simply because they want to do their best. They want to experience their "best self," and they have learned that in attempting to win, they do become their best.

They are not interested in beating you because their desire to win has absolutely nothing to do with you. It is simply their own desire to find out what they can be and do. Therefore, they have no strong emotional response to winning or losing. They realize that nothing is different about them whether they have won or lost. They either learned something about themselves and their ability or they did not. And they are able to quickly make sense of both winning and losing because nothing has changed about who they are.

Let's Not Talk About That

Growing up in the South, we were always told that there were certain things polite people did not talk about in public. This list included religion, politics, money, and, of course, sex.

This greatly disappointed me growing up because I thought these were the most interesting things to talk about and that knowing a person's opinions on these subjects was a quick way to see who they truly were. When I got older and became a psychotherapist, I realized that these were also the subjects that tended to cause people the most pain in their lives and their relationships.

In the field of sports and other competitive arenas, there is one topic that tends to get people riled up more than anything else: winning. Early in my career, I wrote a piece about the importance of winning that I included in a newsletter that I sent out to the university's athletic department. Several people, none of whom were coaches, felt the need to visit me at my office to inform me that I was putting out the wrong message by suggesting that winning was important.

I listened to their opinions and thanked them for sharing their concerns, but ultimately I concluded that they just didn't get it.

So, here I am again, some 20 years later, about to walk out and stand in front of the firing squad with the same message now validated through two decades of research and experience.

Winning is important, really important.

But not for the reasons you might think.

The Real Reason Winning Is Actually Important

The winning I'm talking about is not about scoreboards, trophies, or championships. It's what happens to a person once he or she has the *desire* to win, the *intention* to win, and the *expectation* to win. What I am most interested in is helping people perform at their highest level possible—their full potential. The fact of the matter is that people who have a strong desire to win, to be the best at what they do, are more likely to reach their full potential than someone who says, "I don't care if I win or lose. I just want to get better."

That's why winning matters. It will bring out the best in you and push you to your limits. If winning were more important than getting better, then the best athletes would compete against inferior competition that they knew they could beat, when, in fact, the best competitors want to compete against the best—even if it means possibly losing.

Frequently, I'll ask great athletes who are struggling why they don't just play down a level so they can win again. Inevitably, I get the same response: "I would never do that. There's no way I would step down a level so that I could win."

There's the proof that competing against someone who actually has the ability to beat you is more interesting than competing against someone whom you know you can dominate. Sure, we want to win, but only if there is joy in winning, which means losing has to be a possibility. And there is only joy if your competition is as good as or better than you are.

One of my many complaints about college football is the scheduling. Because the rating system is subjective and biased, and therefore broken, schools have taken to playing teams that are inferior and not valid opponents in order to ensure that they have enough wins to make it to a bowl or actually win the national championship. In other words, many schools play two to three games each year against a far inferior opponent in order to pad their schedule with a couple of extra wins. The inferior schools take the game because the payout is significant, up to $1 million.

The other problem we have with winning is that we like to put the word *the* before the word *winner*, as in, "I am the winner." This terminology suggests that there is only one winner, making everyone else "the loser."

We would be much better off if we put the word *a* before the word *winner*, creating the phrase, "I am a winner." This implies that there is more than one winner. The problem we have in our society of narcissism, thin skin, and self-absorption is that everyone is trying to be *the* winner and not *a* winner.

Can you and I both be winners? This entire dilemma is created out of insecurity and fear. We need to let being "the winner" go and start trying to be "a winner." Your level of performance will improve, and you will also like yourself a lot more.

A Winning Mentality

I have had the good fortune of working with teams, athletes, and companies that cover the full spectrum of the winning-losing continuum. It's inevitable that the teams that expect to win games practice with a level of intensity that other teams can only imagine.

Imagine going to practice or work every day and knowing that the reason you are doing what you do is because you believe that you and your teammates are going to do something really special, something that history will remember for a long time. Your whole life will change when you shift your way of thinking. There is purpose in everything you do. You matter and everyone else matters too. It's probably the most fun and excitement an adult human can legally have. That's why winning matters—it escalates the experience to an optimal level.

Another reason winning matters is that winning creates opportunity. In tournament play, winners advance to the next round while the losers go home. In business, a winner keeps his or her job and makes more money, while a loser becomes unemployed or underpaid.

If you enjoy what you do, doing it well allows you to keep doing it, often along new horizons. Success leads to more choices. Positive attributes are credited to those who succeed at the highest level. I'm not saying this is fair or the way it should be. It's just the way it is.

Employers like to hire candidates who went to prestigious schools or were awarded honors while in college. College coaches prefer an athlete who played for a championship team over one who never played for a winning team. Why? Because we believe that a person who knows how to win, desires to win, and expects to win is a better competitor than one who has not been in an environment with high expectations and a championship culture. I couldn't agree more.

●———●

Years ago, I worked with a team that did not have a history of winning. In fact, they lost more than they won. One day, while meeting with the coach, I asked her how she thought her team would do that year.

"Well, Stan, we are going to try to win every game we play. But, of course, that's not going to happen."

At that point, she lifted up the large calendar on her desk and removed the season's schedule that lay under it. She described to me how before every season, she would take the schedule and predict whether or not her team would win or lose each of their games.

I was pleased that she would trust me with such private information, but I was at the same time surprised by this practice.

"So," I asked, "what happens if you win a game you thought you would lose or lose a game you thought you would win? How does this affect your approach to the season?"

It occurred to me that if the coach didn't really think the team would win, it had to affect the way the coach interacted with the team. There's no doubt in my mind that players know if their coach believes they will win or believes in them as competitors.

The best leaders are the ones who give their organizations the permission to believe that they can win. Teams that win are led by leaders who believe that winning matters and that it's okay to enter into every competition with a positive expectation.

During the course of an athlete's life, there will be times when he or she expects to win and other times when they do not believe they are as good as their competition. Most everyone who reaches the collegiate level of competition has had a point in their career when they wanted to win and believed they would win every time they entered a competition.

However, once they get to the college, Olympic, or professional level, this desire and expectation to win usually becomes unstable and less predictable.

One thing I do with athletes who have lost the belief that they can win is ask them about a time in their career when they expected to and did in fact win. This is not difficult because most of these athletes dominated the competition when they were kids and all the way through high school.

I ask them, "What has changed about you? How are you different now? Have you lost your ability? Are you not as good as you once were?"

Immediately, they realize that they are better now than they were in high school, and a puzzled look comes over their face. They don't know what happened, but I do. They *lost*.

One day they entered a competition with the same expectation they always had, but this time they got beat, and the world has never been the same since. No one ever told them that success is not about *avoiding* failure but about *responding* to failure instead.

If winning is important, then competition has to be important as well. In fact, the approach to competition—how you view the competitive environment—is just as important as winning. The process determines the outcome. How you view competition is the process. The final score is the outcome.

In order to do well in a competitive environment, we must learn to focus on the process and not the outcome. Teams that win at a high rate don't talk that much about winning. They talk about how they want to play the game (the process). Great coaches don't try to fire up their teams by screaming, "Let's go out there and win this game!" Rather, they talk about the things they believe the team needs to do in order to win the game.

Believing you are going to win actually gives you permission to not obsess about winning, and it frees your mind to focus on the here and now. Believing that you will do well keeps your mind free from distractions and anxious thoughts, leaving you with a quiet mind that leads to a great performance.

KEY TAKEAWAY

Winners don't think about winning. They think about what they must do before a competition to be successful, and they do very little thinking during the competition itself. Great competitors know when and how to just *play* the game.

In 1980, Dr. George Sheehan wrote a jewel of a book entitled *This Running Life*. My favorite chapter is a short, three-page chapter entitled "The Spirit." In this chapter, Dr. Sheehan reminds us of the origins of the words *compete* and *contest*.

Compete

Competition holds the promise to bring out the very best in us, and that's why we should seek it out. The word comes from the Latin root *peto*, which means "to go out or to seek." The prefix *com* means "with" or "together." Thus, *competition* is a social process that requires others. You can't do it by yourself.

But what is it that we should seek during competition? Sheehan suggests that "competition is simply each of us seeking our absolute best with the help of each other."

I love that statement. It's one of the best sentences I have ever read in my entire life. It captures the notion that we are not in this competitive world alone. We are all here together struggling for the same things. Sheehan follows that sentence with two more great ones: "What we do magnifies each other, inspires each of us. The race is a synergistic society where what accrues to one accrues to all, a society in which everyone can be a winner."

You want what I want, and I need you in order to achieve my goals. You need me to challenge you so that you can reach your potential. It's poetry.

Great competitors are assisted, not inhibited, by the competition. Going against the best should inspire us, drive us, and set our souls on fire. Competing against the best will bring out the best in you if you learn how to compete *with* and not *against*.

Those who fail to catch the tailwind of competition do so because they compete *against* each other. Great competitors understand the meaning of competing *with* one another.

Contest

As we mentioned earlier, *contest* begins with the prefix *con*, which also means "with." The second syllable, *test*, is the same root as the word *testify*. When we testify, we speak under oath. We make a promise. When we enter a contest, we should make a promise—not only to ourselves, but to everyone present. Sheehan suggests that the promise should be to do our best.

Whatever you do, make some promise or commitment to yourself. Promise yourself that you will not quit when it gets difficult. Promise yourself that you will not hold anything back. Let the contest be the most important thing in your life at the moment. And make sure you keep your promise to yourself.

People who don't make promises make excuses. Get really good at making and keeping your promises so you won't have to make excuses.

●————————●

As I mentioned earlier, the problem most people have with winning is that they think there can only be one winner and the rest are losers. Not true. There is no one definition for winning, and more than one person can win at a time.

Want an example? Here's a story of how four men won the same race:

It was May 1, 2010, at the Stanford University track. The event was the men's 10,000 meters.

Many of the best distance runners in America show up for the Payton Jordan Classic, and there was a lot of excitement before the race this particular year because Alberto Salazar, the coach of the 2010 American record holder, Galen Rupp, had announced that he believed Rupp would break the American record that night. The hotel ballroom had even been reserved so that Nike could host a big party following this record setting event.

I stood at the fence between two of the best distance coaches in the country: Pete Rea and Greg McMillan. It was magic. The stage was set for the most wonderful of human dramas.

Halfway into the race, the leaders were on record pace, and the excitement was building. Everyone watched with the same anticipation that a child has on Christmas Eve.

With just 600 meters to go, Chris Solinsky took off as if he had been launched out of a giant slingshot. Chris was known as a 5,000-meter runner, and he had not been expected to beat Rupp, much less set a new record. Rupp and the others took chase, and the American record was in serious jeopardy of being broken by not one, but *two* runners.

Solinsky crossed the line in 26:59, shattering Rupp's American record, followed by Rupp in fourth place at 27:10, who also broke the previous record of 27:13. Who won? They both did. They both did exactly what they came to do—set a new American record.

The NCAA record was also rewritten that night by Sam Chelanga of Liberty University with a time of 27:08. And to cap off a wonderful race, the Canadian record was broken by Simon Bairu, Solinsky's former college teammate, with a time of 27:23.

One race, four new records. In total, 13 men ran personal bests that evening in the 10,000 meters, and all can tell the story of how they ran in one of the fastest and best 10,000-meter races in the history of track. That night, 13 men got to say, "I am a winner."

13

The Lucky Ones

Do not pray for easy lives. Pray to be stronger men.

—John F. Kennedy

I frequently hear coaches and athletes refer to an event or result as having either "good luck" or "bad luck." *Luck* is apparently this ethereal mass floating about that either comes to us or abandons us at its own pleasure—kind of like a muse to an artist or an angel to a praying child.

It is amazing to me that very accomplished athletes and businesspeople consistently refer to their success as *luck*.

In the book *Good to Great*, author Jim Collins interviews a number of successful businesspeople, and a majority of them state that their tremendous success is due in part to luck or good fortune. What is it, exactly, that they are referring to? Is it possible that when people refer to "luck," they are not talking about the same phenomenon?

I think that's highly likely.

Well, I hate to rain on your parade, but luck is not something that is *out there*. It's *inside you, inside your mind*. Sure, luck exists, but only in

123

your head. It is a creation of your unconscious mind (and sometimes the conscious mind). Basically, it is how you see yourself in relation to the world.

Do you think of yourself as being lucky or unlucky? The truth is, whichever you believe is true is a very big deal. Luck can be your prediction of how you think you are going to perform before an event even begins because most of us have some premonition of how we will perform before an event starts.

Those who view themselves as "lucky" believe they will get a break, while those who view themselves as "unlucky" believe that the breaks will go to others.

●———●

In the fall of 2015, I was working with a professional golfer whose best friend had recently played in a tournament with Jordan Speith. Jordan was having an amazing run; he had won the Masters, and he was the top player on the tour at the time. My client's friend was waiting on the first tee box when Jordan joined his playing partners for the day. They each shook hands, and then Jordan made a comment that made a lasting impression on the other players. He said, "Fellows, let me go ahead and apologize right now. I've been getting a lot of lucky breaks, so don't get mad at me."

During that same time frame, my brother, Steve, went to Phoenix, Arizona, for work. Steve stayed with our old high school friend Tony Phillips. Tony was an amazing athlete in high school, and then he had played Major League Baseball for 18 years. Steve told me that Tony's mindset was one he hadn't encountered in a long time. Tony stated a number of times, "I don't know why it is, but things always work out for me."

Athletes like Jordan and Tony are showing us what is going on inside their brains. We should pay close attention. If you look at either one of these men, you will not notice anything physically remarkable.

Jordan is 6 feet tall and 185 pounds. Tony is small, only 5 feet 10 and 175 pounds. The difference is what they believe about themselves and what they believe is going to happen to themselves in the future. Whether you believe you are "lucky" or that "things are going to work out for me," those are both beliefs about your future. And when you believe the future is going to be fabulous—"things are going to work out for me"—you are transformed in the present. In other words, the **now** is different because of your belief about the future. That is powerful, and most of us don't even recognize the significance of those types of beliefs. Furthermore, we don't understand that we can think that way too, if only we can muster up the confidence to make such a statement.

Imagine how your life would be different if you believed that things would always work out for you. You would have much less worry and stress in your life. Whenever you had a setback, you would understand that it was part of the process as you continued on your journey. And most importantly, if you believed it was all going to work out, you would be able to stay in the moment with a quiet mind, which would allow for your optimal performance.

False Humility

Just turn on ESPN on any given day, and you will hear your favorite athlete say, "I felt really good in warm-ups, and I thought tonight might be special, but I had no idea I was going to set a record tonight. I guess I was kinda lucky."

KEY TAKEAWAY

Successful people think of themselves as lucky. They believe the world is working with them, not against them.

Luck can also be used as a form of false humility. In other words, you can say after a successful performance, "We were so much better than our opponent tonight. They're really just not at our level." Or the more common and socially accepted version, "We were just lucky tonight. They are a great team, and we feel really fortunate to come out of here with a win." *Really?*

Martin Seligman is a psychologist who has studied optimism or luck, and he has written quite prolifically about his findings. Seligman suggests that optimism is essentially a belief system that can be learned and that it can have a significant impact on our lives.

He has discovered that when a particular event happens to us, we automatically attribute this event to either something internal (oneself) or external (the world). We also attribute the outcome to something positive or negative.

As you might imagine, optimistic people attribute positive outcomes to themselves (internal) and negative outcomes to others (external).

Pessimists Versus Optimists

Imagine this: You just played really well in a game, and now you are attempting to make some sense as to why that happened. Now, let's look at the differences between how optimists and pessimists react to this situation:

Optimist: I played well tonight because I worked hard at practice this week and put forth a great effort during the game. (Internal)

Pessimist: We won the game tonight because the referee made a bad call that went our way. (External)

What is the major difference here? It's not just the positive versus negative attitude. It's whether someone places the blame on internal or external forces. If you are an optimist, you are more likely to attribute the negative outcome to something external such as, "They played really well, and all the breaks went their way." But if you are a pessimist, you may think, "I am not very good. I'll never be very good at this."

In order to shift the mindset from pessimist to optimist, the pessimists have to learn to stop blaming themselves for events that are outside their control. The most important thing they need to learn to control is their own attitudes and beliefs about themselves.

KEY TAKEAWAY

What we refer to as "luck" is actually what we believe to be true about ourselves and the world. People who have a positive view of themselves and the world are the recipients of "good luck."

The Role of a Gut Feeling

The idea that you can predict and attribute your success is nothing new and certainly not found only in sports.

When talking with my corporate clients about success, we usually begin with my asking the group this question: "How many of you have ever had the strong feeling while you were sitting in your car, getting ready to go call on a client, that the sales call was going to go well and that you would make a sale?"

Typically, almost every hand in the room immediately goes up. No one even has to think about the answer—they know before I even finish my question.

Of course, being the pain in the butt that I am, I then ask them the reverse: "Have you ever had a bad feeling in your gut, a sense that the sales call was not going to go well and that you would be unsuccessful?"

Again, most hands go up, but this time they don't fly up the way they did the first time. Instead, a few hands are raised, then a few more, and eventually about two-thirds of the group have raised their hand. The remaining one-third are either liars or cowards—or maybe a little of both.

This phenomenon can be referred to as *mental handicapping*. At your favorite race track, there is a person who has the job of *handicapper*. The handicapper's job is to know the horses, jockeys, and trainers and make a prediction of what will happen based on past performances.

The handicapper knows the same things you know—that the past is the best predictor of the future. People don't change much, and neither do horses.

Once someone picks a trajectory, they tend to stay on it. People who have won in the past tend to think they will win in the future. Likewise, the guy who has never won anything has a hard time believing that today is his Lucky Day.

When working with athletes, I ask them what they are preparing for and what they think is going to happen in their competition tomorrow. Commonly, the response is, "I don't know. I hope it goes well." To which I respond, "That's nonsense! You do have an expectation, and I want to hear it."

There are then usually a few rounds back and forth during which they insist that they really have no idea. But they eventually relent and admit that they have been thinking about it quite a bit lately.

I then ask them what they see when they think about the event—what images come to mind. Most admit that the images and thoughts they have are not very positive, and because they are so negative, they try to push them back down into their unconscious.

Some people are very good at this form of mental manipulation. However, if you want to be great at your sport, your business, or your hobby, you have to get a handle on this. It's huge, and it's critical to your future success.

When preparing for anything in life, you are engaged in physical preparation and mental preparation simultaneously. If you are not intentional or conscious in your mental preparation, you will do it unintentionally or unconsciously.

When the outcome is important, you cannot leave this process to chance, though most of us do. It is not uncommon for athletes to not even be able to imagine themselves doing something well or correctly, and if that is the case, how can they ever hope to be successful?

Changing Your Beliefs

I was once asked to assist a college basketball team improve their free throw percentage. One player was particularly poor at shooting free throws, and, unfortunately, he had to shoot a lot of them.

During one of our first sessions, I asked him to close his eyes and imagine himself shooting the shot. He did and said he missed the shot in that scenario. I explained that this was okay and told him to shoot another. He repeated this exercise a number of times without ever being able to imagine himself making a shot.

What this demonstrated was that he thought he was *supposed* to miss the shot, not make it. We would never be able to improve his percentage until we were able to create a mindset in which he thought he was supposed to make the shot and thus expected to make the shot each time.

Players who make more than 80 percent of their free throws generally think that they will make any given single shot. Their self-belief is, "I make my free throws" or "Free throws are an easy shot."

After working with this particular athlete for quite some time, he was eventually able to imagine himself making the shot. It was only after this phase that he was able to improve his free throw percentage.

This is a classic example of how one's belief system dictates performance. In order for you to improve, you must change what you believe is true about yourself and your ability.

KEY TAKEAWAY

You always have an expectation of how you
will perform. If you are not aware of your expectation,
then it is probably negative.

When I was at the University of Virginia sitting in on Bob Rotella's graduate seminar class, Rotella was working with quite a few PGA touring pros. One day in class he posed the question, "At the beginning of every PGA event, approximately 150 golfers qualify to play. Of those 150 golfers, how many expect to win the tournament?"

The responses ranged from "All of them—these are professional golfers" to "About 10." After all of the responses were in, Rotella shared his. He stated that he did not think more than 5 or 6 really believed that they were the one who was supposed to win the tournament.

He outlined the difference between *hoping* to win (which everyone does) and *expecting* to win (which very few do). Essentially, in any competition in which there are multiple entrants (golf, tennis, running, swimming, and so on), the majority of the field does not expect to win.

If you don't expect to win, then you have disqualified yourself before the event even begins. You have handicapped yourself out of having a fair chance to win, and you have given the field a head start and unfair advantage.

KEY TAKEAWAY

Your mental goal should be to expect to win
or do well at whatever sport or task you participate in.

In June 2011, a couple of track coaches I had been working with asked me to attend the USA Track and Field Championships in Eugene, Oregon, to work with their athletes.

I flew to Salt Lake City and jumped on a small commuter plane to Eugene. There were quite a few athletes on the flight, and I found myself sitting next to one. I figured the young man was a sprinter because one of his thighs was the size of both of mine.

We introduced ourselves, and he said he was Justin Gatlin, a sprinter training in Florida. I did not know Justin or that he was a former Olympic gold medalist in the 100 meter in 2004. Nor was I aware that he had won six NCAA titles in two years and had left college after his sophomore year to turn pro. Additionally, I was not aware that he had just completed a four-year ban from the sport because his body evidently produced about as much testosterone as one would normally find at an entire Boy Scout jamboree. Nevertheless, we got to talking, and I shared with him my theory that most runners disqualify themselves before the event even begins because they don't expect to win.

Justin immediately agreed with me and said that in the sprint events, there is usually one—and only one—guy who really thinks he will win. He went as far as to suggest that everyone in the field knows who that person is.

131

I was quite surprised by his candor, and I found his description of how sprinters enter a race to be very interesting and informative. We discussed the phenomenon for quite a while, and I felt privileged to have one of the greatest sprinters of my time share with me what he truly thought was going on in his mind and in the minds of his competitors.

"Well, Justin, what do you expect will happen to you at this meet?" I quipped.

He said that this was his first meet in quite some time (again, I didn't know he was coming off of a drug suspension) and he would be happy with a top three finish, which would qualify him for the world championships later that year. We said our good-byes as we exited the plane, and I realized then that he would not win the event.

Several days later, I watched the finals with great anticipation. The favorite to win (Tyson Gay) withdrew from the competition due to injury, and Justin was now running with a real chance of winning the U.S. championship, something he was not mentally prepared to do.

The gun went off, and Justin established himself in the front of the pack and separated as the field soared toward the finish. For a moment, I thought, "Holy shit! He's going to win the race!"

Although his body crossed the finish line first, Justin didn't win. Instead of leaning forward, he looked to his left to see what the competition was doing—a mistake an Olympic champion shouldn't make. Walter Dix won the race in 9.94; Justin came in second with a 9.95.

As Justin looked to his left, Walter Dix leaned forward to win the race, and Justin got second. It was Justin's race. He was the fastest guy that day, but unfortunately, I don't think he believed he deserved to win—and he surely didn't *expect* to win. If he had, he would have leaned into the tape. Keep in mind that this is an Olympic champion we are talking about. Justin is one of the greatest sprinters ever to compete; he has won hundreds of races.

Think about how crazy this is. The majority of athletes never give themselves a chance to win because they have no expectation of winning or don't believe they deserve to win. If such an athlete were in a position to win a tournament, he or she would almost certainly choke in the end because they would find themselves in a position where they did not believe they belonged.

We all withdraw to a place of comfort, a position where we think we truly belong. If you don't believe you deserve it, it probably will not happen.

KEY TAKEAWAY

It isn't luck that determines your success. It's expectation.

Your expectation is the determinant—not your coach, your mom, or your teammates, but you. It's true that you get what you settle for. Whether you think you are lucky or unlucky, you're right!

14

•————————————•

The Value of Time

*Everybody should do at least two things each
day he hates to do, just for practice.*

—WILLIAM JAMES

I n my time as a sport psychologist, I have watched a lot of practices. I have observed that practice varies greatly from coach to coach. They value and use time differently, and there is a noticeable difference in how each one responds to failure and mistakes.

Some coaches know how to create a high-pressured and intense practice environment that simulates competition. Other personalities lead to a more relaxed and focused practice. Still others are experts at creating drills or making the monotony of swimming endless laps interesting.

The best coaches I've seen all have something in common—they understand that the purpose of practice is to prepare for competition. For a competitive athlete, everything, and I mean everything, you do in practice should be to prepare for competition. Great athletes and coaches think about competition during practice. They don't think of practice as separate from competition.

How the Best Teams Use Their Time

During all of the hours that I watched practices, I began noticing how time was valued. The best teams utilized their time more efficiently. At the time (and this is still the case today), the National Collegiate Athletic Association (NCAA) had limitations on the amount of time a team could practice each week. Therefore, the better the coaches utilized their time, the faster their team would develop. If a drill or activity did not allow the team to perform better in competition, it was removed and replaced with something that addressed a specific deficit observed during competition.

The teams that didn't succeed of course still had practices, but they weren't organized to maximize time, and they didn't include activities that the athletes believed were helping them get better.

The great coaches explain two things at their practices: why certain things are done and the intended outcome of each activity. Once athletes understand why they are doing something, they are better able to fully engage in the activity. When they are not able to understand the purpose of specific activities, they will fail to fully engage in the activity.

KEY TAKEAWAY

Everyone has the same amount of time, but successful people value their time more, and thus they are more efficient.

During my first year working at the collegiate level, I worked with many different teams, but there was one coach in particular who had not asked me to help with his team. One day I ran into this coach, and he asked me to come and watch his practice. I agreed. After watching the first hour, I left to go attend another practice. This went on for an entire week.

He never talked to me during practice. In fact, he never even acknowledged that I was there. I came, I watched, I left. The following week, he called and asked me to come to his office.

"What do you think?" he asked.

"About what?"

"The practice. What did you think about our practice?"

"Coach, I watch a lot of practices, and your practices are the quietest practices I have ever seen," I told him. "You are the only one who talks. In fact, I can't even remember hearing your assistant coaches talk."

He seemed surprised by my answer, but I could tell he was thinking about what I had just said. The fact that he had allowed me to come to his practice told me that he had a concern or problem he was unable to figure out himself. Yet, he never asked for help. He just wanted my attendance and attention.

"Can I ask you question, Coach?"

"Sure. Fire away."

"How would you assess the quality of leadership on your team? Do you have good leadership from any of your players?"

"That's a good question," he said. "I don't think I have *any* leaders on this team, and that's one of the things that bother me."

"Why do you think you don't have any leaders?"

"I'm not sure. I mean, I have some ideas, but I'm not positive. Some of these athletes were really good leaders in high school, but they just haven't stepped up in college."

I asked him if he wanted to hear my thoughts on the subject.

"Yeah," he said. "That's why I asked you to watch practice. I didn't want to tell you what the problem was because I thought it would bias your opinion."

"Well, Coach, I appreciate your letting me come and watch, and yes, I do have some thoughts regarding your leadership problem. But I gotta be honest," I said. "I don't think you're going to like me after I tell you what I think is the problem. Are you sure you want me to go on?"

"Hell, yes! Go on. I'm not going to get mad at you. You're trying to help us right?"

"Yeah, that's my intention—to help you. But in order to help you, I have to offend you first." I paused to let him digest that last comment. "The reason you don't have any leaders is because you don't create the space for anyone else to assert themselves. You are the only one who talks in practice. The assistant coaches and all of the athletes are looking to you for what to do next. I noticed this during your games too. If you want to have leaders, you have to let them lead. You have to give them some room to step up."

Coaches need to ask captains or team leaders to address the team at practice, before games, and even during games. The same is true in corporate America. The best CEOs have their VPs and managers speak during meetings and even in front of the entire company. A secure leader makes it about the team or organization. An insecure leader makes it about himself or herself.

How to Use Your Time

During the year that led up to the 1996 Olympics, I had the opportunity to watch a couple of Olympians practice over the course of about a year. The Georgia coach had become good friends with a coach in Cincinnati who had two Olympic gymnastics hopefuls in her gym: Amanda Borden and Jaycee Phelps.

They were both great kids from great families. Not only did Amanda and Jaycee make the 1996 Olympic team, they also won gold medals. It was a great experience for everyone involved.

Before this, I had been observing collegiate gymnasts during practice, and I had noticed how individual gymnasts utilized their time. Gymnastics is very different from almost all other sports in that the athletes have a lot of control over how they use their time and what events they focus on in a given practice. My primary focus was calculating how much of an athlete's time was spent training versus how much of the athlete's time was spent preparing or transitioning between events. Gymnastics is about repetition; whoever gets the most reps in during a practice has a competitive advantage.

What I learned was shocking. The majority of the girls spent less than 10 minutes per hour actually training. The remaining time was mostly spent getting prepared or transitioning. At UGA, it was not uncommon to observe a gymnast spending 5 minutes or less per hour in actual training. And these were not only some of the best gymnasts in the country but it was one of the best teams as well!

I tried this same observation technique in Cincinnati and saw similar results. But then I observed Amanda Borden utilize 20 minutes in one hour. That was the most productive gymnastics practice session I ever saw, and it proved why she became a gold medalist.

Several years ago, I read Malcom Gladwell's book *Outliers*, which examines how people achieve greatness. Gladwell claims that in addition to natural talent and fortunate timing, one must also put in 10,000 hours of practice in order to achieve greatness.

When I read this, I immediately thought of all the time I had spent watching practices, and I realized that this had been my observation as well, except that I would add that while a lot of practice was necessary to become great, if that practice was not productive, it would take much longer to reach greatness—if it was ever reached at all. The simple fact is that the more productive, competition-like reps you can get in a practice, the faster you get better.

You have to actually *practice* better if you want to *get* better.

PART III

Become the Person
You Want to Be

15

Be ... Do ... Have

*It isn't sufficient just to want. You've got to ask yourself
what you are going to do to get the things you want.*

—Franklin D. Roosevelt

s I've said earlier, when I am working with a new client, I often
ask them this simple question: "What do you want?" Surprisingly, most people struggle to come up with an answer.

It's a fairly simple and straightforward question, isn't it? So, answer
it right now. Put the book down, get a sheet of paper, and write down
your answer to the question: *What do you want?*

It's harder than you think, isn't it? Most people struggle to answer
this simple question because the fact of the matter is they don't know
what they want. Furthermore, they don't think they could have what
they wanted even if they knew what they wanted.

Have, Do, and Be

When I see a person struggling with the "what do you want?" question, I give them a little help by adding words to the sentence. At this point, I usually put the pyramid shown in Figure 15.1 on a sheet of paper or a white board.

Have

So, let me re-ask you the question this way: *What do you want to have?*

"Oh, now I get it," they respond. "I want to have more money, a bigger house, a new car, a better job . . ." and off they go like they are sitting on Santa's lap. Everyone has a wish list of things they want, and most believe that if they had those things, their life would be better.

Figure 15.1   What Do You Want?

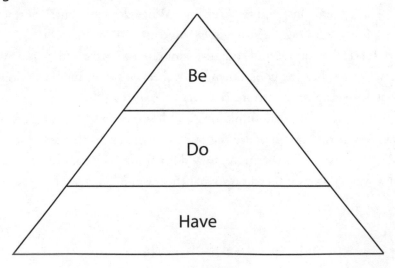

Do

Next, I write the word "Do" in the middle section of the pyramid.

Let me ask you the question a little differently this time: *What do you want to* do*?* How do you like to spend your time? What are the activities you enjoy the most?

Most of us are able to answer this question, but some find it harder than the first. There are typically fewer answers and more time between responses. It usually goes something like, "I want to spend more time with my kids, work less, and travel more . . . "

The first question is about material things—stuff. But this question of "what do you want to do?" is about how you wish to spend your *time*. What is more valuable to you, your stuff or your time? Be honest. Would you move into a smaller house so you could spend more time with your kids? Would you drive a used car in order to travel to the places you always wanted to go? Unfortunately, most of us value our stuff more than we value our time.

So, how do people who achieve greatness answer these questions? Do they value stuff or time more? That's right; they value time more than money or material goods. But you knew that already, didn't you?

Be

Next, I write the word "Be" in the top triangle of the pyramid. The final question to this trilogy is: *What do you want to be?* Think about it, who are you? It's an important question to be able to answer. But first you must answer, "What am I now?"

"Who am I?" is the most important and difficult of all questions to answer. When I ask people this question, the vast majority are unable to answer it. "Who am I?" is present tense. "What do I want to be?" is future tense. You have to know who you are now in order to become the person you want to be.

It's kind of like reading a map—in order to figure out how to get somewhere, you have to locate your present position as well as the place you are trying to go. If the first question is about material things, and the second question is about time, the third question is about character. It's about *you*. Remember this is the "Who am I?" question. This question is about telling yourself the truth about whom and what you are.

Putting It All Together

If you have not reached your full potential but want to, then you must first acknowledge that you have not reached your full potential. Understanding the relationship between the "do" and the "be" is imperative, and how you spend your time is absolutely critical to what you want to be.

I encourage people to forget about what they want to have or possess—it's a waste of time. The same goes for awards and honors. Forget about them. They will not help you improve your performance. Instead, become obsessed with how you spend your time, the choices you make, and who you hang out with. Kids, you should measure the amount of time you spend working out, reading, doing homework, playing video games, etc. Adults, you should measure the amount of time you spend at work, in traffic, talking to your kids, waiting at the airport, etc. Because how you spend your time will dictate what (and who) you ultimately become.

● —— ●

My friend and former priest, Paul Winton, once told a group of us, "Show me your checkbook and calendar, and I will know who you are." In other words, you can measure a person by how they spend their money and their time. I couldn't agree more.

The consumerism doctrine is that the desire for things leads to the desire for more things. The high performance doctrine is different. It says that the desire to use your time more effectively leads to a better person. In other words, true desire leads to doing that which leads to a better being.

16

•————————•

The Seeker

*Most people never run far enough on their first
wind to find out they've got a second. Give your
dreams all you've got, and you'll be amazed
at the energy that comes out of you.*

—WILLIAM JAMES

Running is physical. Racing is mental.

Have you ever been to a horse race? The energy and excitement of watching those huge animals run so fast are quite dramatic. Yet there is a lot of strategy and planning involved in running and winning a horse race. The favorites usually win, as is true with humans, and both have numerous components involved in the outcome.

In horse racing, you have three major components: the horse, the trainer, and the jockey. Horses want to run, and they will run to the point of injury if left to their own accord (which sounds just like humans). That's where the trainer comes in. The trainer controls almost every aspect of the horse's life: when he runs, how much he runs, how fast he runs, how much he eats, who rides the horse, and so on. The jockey is responsible for the horse's behavior while he's on the horse's back.

Before the race, the jockey must be relaxed and confident, which in turn helps the horse to be the same. Once the race starts, the jockey must ensure that the horse does not go out too fast, and the jockey must position the horse on the track so that the horse will not be encumbered by other horses during the race.

When gamblers go to the track, they assess all three—the horse, the trainer, and the jockey—before placing a bet. If one component is missing, the horse will not race well.

Now, let's apply this analogy to humans racing. Your physical body is the equivalent of the horse. Your coach and/or training regimen is the equivalent to the trainer. And your mind or mental state is the jockey. Before the race, you should attend to your physical state and training. But once the race begins, you must be the jockey, not the horse. Your job is to go as fast as you possibly can on that given day.

Training is a physical act. It involves the movement of your body, the conditioning, and the nutrition you have to make your body go. Competing, on the other hand, is primarily a mental activity. It is your ability to use your mind to maximize your body's ability.

What you believe you can do and how you are going to do it all come into play in racing. Great competitors don't run against the competition—they run *with* the competition.

●———————●

In the world-famous *Harry Potter* series written by J.K. Rowling, Harry plays a most unusual game called Quidditch. Harry and six teammates fly around on their brooms chancing after one of four balls. The position Harry plays is Seeker, and his role role is catching the smallest of the balls, the Golden Snitch, before the other team's Seeker does.

While Quidditch is a game played in a world filled with magic, the name of Harry's position makes you think. What should we be seeking during competition? The answer is: *the best of ourselves*.

The purpose of competition is to perform at our very best. Great competitors use the competition to help them perform at their best, like a jockey putting his horse in perfect position to win. On the other hand, poor competitors are only inhibited by the competition.

It's amazing how a given situation can bring out the best in one person and the worst in another.

Being a great competitor means that you are able to use the other competitors to help you run fast, not to hinder you. The sole purpose of everyone else in the race is to help you run faster. The person in front of you is simply showing you what is possible. They are saying, "You can do this!"

The desire to win, to be the best in a given moment of time, is a concept that makes many of us uncomfortable. The fact of the matter is that the desire or intention to win will bring out the best in you. You should want to win because it will lead you to your best, not because you will triumph over another.

The world's greatest competitors have a tremendous respect and love for their fellow competitors. They know that they are dependent on them and they need them in order to do well enough to find the best within themselves. This tension, this struggle, helps create the transformation that great athletes seek. They compete primarily because they desire to be fulfilled and complete—not because they wish dominance over another.

In the end, athletes who compete with the primary desire to be better than someone else—rather than being better than their previous self—will never find their best. It is ultimately *you* whom you are competing against. It is who you are now versus who you could be that will make you successful.

The Latin root of the word *contest* means "to testify with or to make a promise with." I love what this suggests. Imagine if every time you entered a contest, the promise you made was to do your best. That's all you can do anyway. It is very unsatisfying and even frustrating to watch a competition in which the athletes are not trying to do their best. In fact, it is quite a rare thing to see athletes giving it all they have. The majority almost always hold a little something back.

Have you ever driven by a store and seen the sign: "Liquidation Sale—All Items Must Go"? That's what every race should be, a liquidation sale. Everything goes. Everything. When the race is over, you should be empty. Hollow. Spent. Done. Nothing left.

Once you are empty, all that is left is contentment. The only way one can be fully satisfied after a race is to be empty. If you leave anything in reserve, you will be haunted by it until you can race again.

Performing at the highest level is not about talent, ability, size, speed, facilities, equipment, weather conditions, or even effort. It's about being free. Free from expectations of self and others, free from criticism, free from fear, and free from "should" and "have to."

There are many routes to success. So you shouldn't be overly invested in a specific outcome or result. If you are, this will bite you in the butt every time. Freedom means no attachments, no desires, just one very quiet mind that allows you to perform to the best of your natural abilities that have been instilled in you during intentional practice.

When athletes have a great performance, they frequently find themselves being interviewed after the competition. The interviewer asks a series of questions to discern how they did it. "What were you thinking about?" "How did it feel to make that shot at the buzzer?" Usually the athletes start and stop a number of times because quite frankly, they don't know the answers to the questions. Their mind was not thinking. They were reacting, seeing, feeling, but definitely not thinking. In most cases, they won't be able to tell you what happened or how they did it. Instead, it just happened. There is very little memory of the event, and time and space tend to be distorted as well. It was absence, not presence that had allowed the wonderful to happen.

You must trust yourself and your ability in order to perform at that level. Ultimately, you can't *will* yourself to greatness, but you can *trust* yourself to greatness if you've done your preparation.

17

• ———————————— •

A Monk's Character and Commitment

*If I were dropped out of a plane into the ocean
and told the nearest land was 1,000 miles away, I'd
still swim. And I'd despise the one who gave up.*

—ABRAHAM MASLOW

The greatest endurance athletes in the world are not even athletes—they're Buddhist monks living on Mount Hiei in Japan.

For them, there is no competition to win, no competitor to beat, no trophy to hoist, and no lucrative contract to sign. The 1,000 marathons they complete over seven years are viewed as a meditation, not a competition. The goal is personal transformation and enlightenment—not just for themselves but for others as well.

What they do is amazing, but what they *don't* do is even more incredible.

These monks don't just complete a marathon; they walk/run 1,000 marathons over seven years. To put this in perspective, the monks walk

The 1,000-Day Mountain Marathon by Year

First year	100 days	40K each day
Second year	100 days	40K each day
Third year	100 days	40K each day
Fourth year	2 × 100 days	40K each day
Fifth year	2 × 100 days	40K each day

The Greatest Fast: Nine Days of No Food, Water, or Rest

Sixth year	100 days	60K each day
Seventh year	100 days	84K each day
	100 days	40K each day

Sources: John Stevens, *The Marathon Monks of Mount Hiei*, Echo Point Books, Brattleboro, Vermont, 2013. Documentary written by Christopher Haden, published by DER Documentary, 2002.

farther than the equatorial circumference of the earth. They travel 46,572 kilometers—the earth is 40,075 kilometers (or 24,901 miles).

It's one of those things that while you actually watch it, a part of your brain is telling you that this can't be true—that it's impossible. It was amazing to me then, and after researching the monks and their lives, it is even more amazing to me now.

As Westerners, we have developed a belief system that suggests to us what is humanly possible and what is not. Our belief system dictates what we believe we are capable of and what we're not, in addition to what we should attempt and what we should leave alone.

Our unconscious mind dictates every aspect of our human lives, but what if this system is wrong? What if more is possible than we believe? What if Western science does not have all of the answers regarding human potential? What if our culture, science, and belief systems are actually keeping us from reaching our potential and even limiting our performance? Are you willing to change your mind? In order to achieve greatness, you'll have to.

KEY TAKEAWAY

What you believe is the most important thing in
the world to you. Your beliefs about what
is possible and impossible will dictate your
behavior and, ultimately, your success.

The Rules of the Mountain

While on the marathon, the monks must follow many rules. Their robes and hats may not be removed. They are not allowed to change or deviate from the course. No stopping is allowed for rest or refreshment, although there is one appointed stop where the monks are allowed to sit in order to pray. All prayers, meditations, and chants must be performed correctly, and absolutely no smoking or drinking alcohol is allowed.

Most monks sleep about four to five hours a night during the first few years. However, during longer marathons, the monks are limited to less sleep each night. If for some reason the marathon takes longer than expected, monks may get no sleep at all before having to begin the cycle over again.

Symbolism is present throughout the seven-year challenge. Japanese tradition dictates that one puts his sandals on *outside* of the house. Yet, each morning, the monks put their sandals on *inside* the house, which means they have no intention of returning to their home.

Once they begin the process, the monks commit to completing the first 100 days or they must take their own life. Because their Buddhist religion believes in reincarnation and multiple incarnations for a given soul, they view death differently from the way those in the Western world view it. Consequently, their fear of death is nonexistent. To ensure their commitment to completing the marathons, the monks carry both a piece of rope (to hang themselves) and a suicide knife. Along the course, there are a number of markers signifying where previous monks have perished along the way to remind them of the severity of their commitment.

KEY TAKEAWAY

The impossible is done by those who are willing to risk it all.
Those who risk the most achieve the most.

Each monk must ask his superior for permission to walk-jog the marathon. Therefore, because it is self-initiated, they believe they have no right to complain for any reason. Complaining is viewed as a sign of a weak heart. (Read that last sentence again!)

As one monk explained, "The more you suffer, the more pleasure you feel. For us, the fact that there is pain simply means we must discover a way to overcome it. If you find the walk painful, you shouldn't have set out. Pain does not really matter. It is only a symptom of the effort you are putting into the task."

The individual and his accomplishments are not significant. Instead, it is being allowed to continue the tradition that matters most. The monk does not view the marathon as something he is doing for himself. He is doing this for the benefit of others, both past and present. The response the monks have for being allowed to complete the marathon is simply *gratitude*.

Buddhists believe that one of the greatest accomplishments individuals can achieve is to truly know themselves and that there should be no limits to what they can and should do to be successful in the attempt to become fully aware.

Adversity and the real possibility of death have a powerful way of introducing one to oneself. In great adversity and challenge, a person sees oneself the clearest. You can fake it when things are going well, but that strategy will surely fail once hope is lost.

KEY TAKEAWAY

Increased self-awareness leads to improved performance. Physical and psychological challenges are essential to one's development because they show us who we truly are. Seek out difficult experiences while your competitors avoid them.

Hoko zen is a form of walking meditation. The marathon monks view the marathon as a meditation and a form of transformation rather than a physical exercise. They believe there are only three basic human desires: food, water, and rest. Therefore, the Great Fast (year 5) consists of nine days without meeting the basic human desires.

Though modern science suggests that humans can live only seven days without food or water, by withholding these basic needs, these monks believe they can overcome them. By doing so, they are no longer attached to these desires. (Monks lose about 25 percent of their total body weight during the fast.)

The Story of Sakai

From 1885 to 1988, only 46 men (*gyoja*) have completed the 1,000-day marathon. Two of these spiritual athletes have completed the 1,000-day challenge twice, the most famous being Sakai.

Today, Sakai remains the most well known and respected of all the marathon monks. However, his path to Mount Hiei is not what you might expect. He reports that when he was a child, he did poorly in school, often failing his exams. As a young man, he was a member of the military, and during World War II, he belonged to a unit that used biological weapons to kill large numbers of Chinese people.

After the Japanese lost the war, Sakai married a cousin who later committed suicide. His family then opened a noodle shop, which burned down soon thereafter. Sakai became depressed and saw no purpose in his life, so he joined the monks of Mount Hiei with a desire to turn his life around.

"I was lazy and had a good-for-nothing life," he said.

During his first 1,000-day marathon (Sennichi Kaihogyo), Sakai became exhausted and was certain he was destined to die. Instead of carrying the symbolic coin all *gyoja* carry, Sakai began to carry the equivalent of several hundred dollars so that whoever found his body could arrange for a proper funeral.

One day, while walking the Kaihogyo in the winter, Sakai was attacked and injured by a wild boar, later developing a very painful infection in his foot. While he initially ignored the wound, his first two toes soon swelled to twice their normal size and turned a deep purple.

Aware of his promise to complete the marathon, he lanced the wound with his suicide knife and thought he might pass out from the pain. Sakai held the knife in front of him so that when he lost consciousness, he would impale himself and end his life.

Fortunately, when he woke up, he realized he had fallen to the side and did not actually impale himself with his own knife. Encouraged by the fact that he was still alive, he got up and continued the 1,000-day challenge.

"I did not know how or why, but I survived. Fate intervened," he said.

Sakai believed that he had accessed a higher power. Learning that the reliance on human strength alone was limiting, he was propelled by a force unknown to most.

Sakai frequently expressed his desire to die while performing the first Kaihogyo. Feeling that he had not yet achieved the discipline he sought to acquire, he began a second tour soon after completing the first. Sakai increased his mileage so that he could complete the practice in six years instead of the normal seven. By the time he finished his second 1,000-day marathon challenge, he was 61. All of this was accomplished on a 1,500-calorie vegetarian diet and with only about three hours of sleep each night.

Afterward, Sakai said, "Human life is like a candle. If it burns out halfway, it does no one any good. I want the flame of my practice to consume my candle completely, letting that light illuminate thousands of places. My practice is to live wholeheartedly, with gratitude and without regret."

Years after his journey, Sakai shared this advice in an interview: "The message I wish to convey is please, live each day as if it were your entire life. If you start something today, finish it today. Tomorrow is another world."

In 2004, a monk named Fujinami completed the marathon under the direction of Sakai. Soon after he finished, he reported, "I feel I have accomplished a job; that is all. I do not know whether I should call it enlightenment or not, but the training has taught me that everyone and everything is equal. A human being is not special; there are no special things."

John Stevens is an American who has studied the marathon monks and spent time with them on Mount Hiei. In his book *The Marathon Monks of Mount Hiei*, Stevens shares an interesting insight into their lives. The insight gives the rest of us hope in attaining our own lofty, seemingly impossible goals.

He states that the monks believe that if you train, no matter what the task, you can accomplish it. The monks believe in bringing out their Buddha nature or spirit, which in turns allows them to reach their full potential. If they do not access their divinity, the God within, they will not be able to realize their true selves and potential.

The monks don't do these things for attention or fame—they do them in isolation. Once you get your ego out of the way (the need to be "special"), you become free, and you can reach your true potential. Doing something for attention or accolades will actually hinder your progress. Through their commitment, they show us all what our capacity is as human beings.

●————●

As a society, we tend to separate our physical, psychological, and spiritual health into different compartments. However, the monks live as if these are all connected; what happens in one area affects the others. In other words, there is a spiritual and psychological component to physical activity. Physical suffering can lead to spiritual enlightenment and greater self-awareness.

As your body becomes stronger, you change psychologically as well. And when you push yourself physically to the edge, this can lead to a spiritual awakening in some people—especially when they feel there is a force outside of themselves assisting them.

The primary lesson from the monks is one of commitment. When you commit to doing something, do it! Don't make excuses. Don't renegotiate. Just do what you said you would do—as if your life depended on it.

If you are really willing to sacrifice yourself in this way, over and over again, you can achieve some amazing things. Most of us tend to hold a little back in reserve, not fully committing to anything. But if you fully commit yourself, the impossible truly becomes possible.

18

What's Fun Got to Do with It?

Just play. Have fun. Enjoy the game.

—Michael Jordan

Throughout my career, some college coaches have allowed me to come in on a regular basis and meet with their players without the coaches' being present. This is a big deal because collegiate coaches are typically very protective of their players, and they tightly control who has access to them.

I was given access to a baseball team that was into their second season and struggling to find success in their conference, which was a very competitive league. During one of our weekly meetings, I could see that the tension was very high in the room.

One of the athletes had shared with me during an individual session that the cause of the tension was twofold: two of the guys were fighting over a girl, and the team had lost a couple of close games they should have won. Furthermore, there was a lack of confidence in the coach's ability to help them get past these events.

At the beginning of the meeting, I asked the team how things were going and what they wanted to discuss during the session. The response was dead silence.

"Anyone have anything they want to say?" I asked. More silence.

So I just sat with them in the quiet, knowing that eventually the pressure would build to a point where someone would blow. Finally, one of the better athletes blurted out, "This isn't any fun. Playing baseball has always been where I have fun, and for the first time, I hate it. I hate coming to practice, I hate the games—I just hate it."

Silence again.

"How about the rest of you?" I asked. "Does anyone else feel the same way?"

Surprisingly, almost all of the hands in the room went up. The men looked around at each other. Finally, one of those who didn't raise his hand said, "But we're not here to have fun. We're here to win games."

"What's the difference?" I asked him. "What's the difference between having fun and winning?"

"I don't understand your question."

I then asked everyone in the room to think of what team they were on when they had the *most* fun playing baseball—any team, any age, any level. I told them to raise their hands when they had their answers.

In less than 10 seconds, every hand in the room was in the air.

I then went around, and I asked each of them to tell me about that very fun team—how old they were, whom they played with, who their coach was, and finally, what their win-loss record was.

The majority of the men told a story of a championship team that had entered each game expecting to win. After five or six players told their stories in detail, I asked the group, "Does anyone see a trend developing here?"

"Sure," said the guy who had first started the discussion. "Winning is fun. Losing sucks."

"There you go! If you all want to have fun playing baseball, you're going to have to find a way to win. There's nothing fun about public embarrassment, making mistakes, and playing below your ability. In a competitive sport, you cannot separate the process from the outcome."

The same is true for almost everything in life. People who enjoy their work have better relationships with colleagues and are more productive than those who don't. Winning will always be fun because winning is associated with playing toward your highest ability. Likewise, losing will always be frustrating because it is associated with fear, lost opportunities, careless errors, and tension.

In business, making money is more enjoyable than losing money. Losing creates intrapersonal tension (such as anxiety and anger) and interpersonal conflicts (such as tension between colleagues and not meeting deadlines).

The Gallup organization has conducted some very good research that demonstrates the correlation between the process and outcome at work. They have defined *employee engagement* as the psychological and interpersonal experiences people have at work. Not surprisingly, the research shows that those who have close friends at work, enjoy the tasks they perform, and believe their company's mission is important are more likely to have a higher rate of production than employees who do not. This higher rate of production, and thus engagement, leads to increased profits for the companies who can create such environments.

Despite the common sense and empirical credibility of such research, we continue to disregard its importance and value. If you like the people you work with and feel that you are well suited for the work you are doing, you will perform at a higher rate than those who don't. Yet, I still hear leaders say, "I don't care if you like me," or "We're not here to have fun—we're here to get the work done." The truth is that fun and success cannot be separated. Process and outcome are intimately related. You get both, or you get neither.

Don't get me wrong—I like being happy and having fun just as much as the next guy, and when things are going my way, I like it. I think that's "fun." But be very aware of the fact that the search for fun will not make any of us great. Instead, what makes us great is the search for *truth*, and the truth is usually painful.

The Importance of the Truth

Seeing yourself as you really are can be humbling and deflating. People who pursue fun are usually willing to tell you (and themselves) a lie in order to keep the fun going. The few who pursue greatness will tell themselves the truth even though it burns down to the bone. They will tell you the truth too, even if it hurts.

Great managers, coaches, teachers, and parents all have something in common: they will tell you the truth even if it hurts. That's the price we all must pay for greatness. You have to want it to be difficult—even more than you want it to be fun. Do that and the fun (a.k.a. winning) will continue.

KEY TAKEAWAY

The truth may hurt, but it never harms.

To Pursue or Not to Pursue

Frequently I hear someone mention one of the best known phrases in the English language. In the Preamble to the Declaration of Independence, it states that we as Americans have the right to "Life, Liberty, and the pursuit of Happiness." This statement leads one to question: How do we actually *gain* happiness or success?

I have noticed that my moments of greatest happiness have not occurred after I have pursued happiness. In fact, my greatest moments of happiness were found when I wasn't looking for or pursuing it. It has also become evident that success is not best achieved by pursuing success. Success, as happiness, is more like a symptom than a goal. Success is the result of pursuing those activities that let us feel most alive, most complete. In fact, I believe that the more we pursue success, the less likely we are to find it. We should pursue those things that allow us to feel the most alive and connected to those around us.

19

Doing the Impossible

*There are two ways to live: you can live as if nothing is a miracle;
or you can live as if everything is a miracle.*

—ALBERT EINSTEIN

Several years ago, I read a biography of St. Francis of Assisi. At the time, I had no idea that a man who died almost eight hundred years before I was born would cause me to leave my home and travel halfway across the world just so I could walk where he walked, sleep where he had slept, and pray where he had prayed.

Because of my schedule, December was the only time I could make the pilgrimage. My Italian friends discouraged me from going in the winter, but I was determined. It took seven days to walk from Rieti to Assisi. It rained almost every day and even sleeted and snowed on me, but I have no regrets. Here's why. Francis was born in 1182 to a wealthy family in Assisi, Italy. In his early years, he was no different from most of his buddies. He played hard and was the life of the party wherever he went. His desire was to become a knight and be respected for his courage and honor.

During a battle with a neighboring town, Francis was captured and taken prisoner. He remained incarcerated for about a year, malnourished and suffering with malaria, until his family paid a ransom to have him released.

Francis would never be the same. He simply could not go back to living a life that didn't matter.

His eyes were opened, and he clearly saw the injustices that he had looked past in his youth. He saw the power and corruption of the church and the lost opportunity that had overtaken an organization that took its constituency for granted.

While praying in the dilapidated chapel of San Damiano, Francis believed he heard God speak to him, and the message he heard was clear: "Rebuild my church."

Francis viewed this as his life's mission, and he went to work rebuilding the church where he had been praying. He would spend the next two years rebuilding three deteriorating chapels near Assisi, though he had no formal training as a builder, no money to buy materials, and no place to sleep. It didn't matter. He was a man on a mission; he pursued his calling with all his heart, mind, and energy.

KEY TAKEAWAY

If you want to live a great life, do what
you are capable of, every day.

The Necessary and Impossible

Reading about St. Francis, one cannot help but be amazed by how much he accomplished, how many lives he affected, and how much influence he had over his generation and those to follow. He became *the* most influential person of his century.

What is even more amazing is that he did this while having no position of power or authority and with only the clothes on his back. Francis voluntarily chose poverty and required all who joined him in the early Franciscan movement to take a vow of poverty also. They were told to sell everything they owned, give the money to the poor, and go live with him.

While still alive, he eventually lost control over the order he founded because he was unwilling to lower his standards and principles. Nevertheless, his ability to accomplish so much in only 20 years made me want to seek out the secret to his success firsthand. Francis did not leave behind much in the way of writings, so it took quite a bit of reading before I finally came across what I believe captures the genius and passion of St. Francis of Assisi:

> First do what is necessary.... Then do the possible.... And then you will find yourself doing the impossible.

To me, this quote undoubtedly represents how Francis was able to achieve tremendous success and affect so many people.

First Do What Is Necessary

When you are beginning a task, a day, a job, or even something that feels impossible, just do what you can. That's what *necessary* means. Do the "have-to" stuff first; complete your to-do list.

You may spend years of your life just doing the necessary, and there is no shame in that. Remember: Francis spent the first two years of his new life gathering and stacking rocks as he rebuilt three chapels.

Master the basics of your craft, business, or sport. Focus on the fundamentals. I have made a pretty good living telling people things they already know. I'm just a reminder. Doing the necessary enables you to move to the next stage

Then Do the Possible

Once you have mastered the basics, the fundamentals, it's time to challenge yourself to see what you are truly capable of: the *possible*. Doing the possible is fully within your reach and ability. You are not being asked to become something you are not. You are to simply become all that you already are. The possible requires your full attention and full commitment, and it requires your unwillingness to go backward to the safety of necessary.

Most of the people in business today believe that each day they go to work and do their very best, which is the possible. Not true. My observations are that most of us do the necessary and then tell ourselves we are doing the possible.

Think about it: Most employees complete their job requirements or their to-do list and stop there. Have you ever heard someone say, "That's not my job," or "That's not my responsibility," or "I don't get paid to do that"? That's the problem with most of us! We believe that we are doing the possible when we go to work and do our very best. But we aren't. Instead, we are doing what's *necessary* and then telling ourselves we are doing the possible.

KEY TAKEAWAY

There is more danger in overestimating
your performance than underestimating it.

You will never perform to your ability if you think the necessary is the possible. The best thing you can do to improve your performance is to think you are doing worse than you actually are, not better.

That's what Francis did. He constantly required more of himself. He never believed that he and his brothers were doing all they could.

Francis was never satisfied, and this belief allowed him to do more than what most would think was possible.

And Once You Realize This, You Will Find Yourself Doing the Impossible

The mystery and magic of this lesson comes in that statement alone. If you commit to doing all that is possible each and every day, a wonderful and marvelous thing will happen to you. You will have the ability to make the impossible possible simply by doing the possible. Notice what changes in this: not the world, but *you*.

20

·————————·

The Hero of Your Own Journey

Courage is being scared to death . . . and saddling up anyway.

—John Wayne

Everyone makes excuses. "I could be a great runner if it weren't for this damn asthma." "The pain in my knee has really interrupted my training." "I have to get my diet figured out." As long as you have a good excuse as to why you haven't started to fly, you never will.

You've got to get rid of the excuses. They are not your friend, and they are not your path to success. Excuses are the damn boogeyman, stalking you, haunting you, and hiding under your bed so that you pull the covers up over your face.

So, what is the real problem?

Fear.

Fear

Fear is what keeps you from being fully motivated, passionate, and driven and setting big hairy-assed goals. If you had no fear, you would be motivated. If you were fearless, you would be driven and running around with your hair on fire. If you weren't scared, you would be taking over the world, and everyone else would get in line behind you.

Fear is your real opponent, not some East African who never owned a pair of shoes until he got a scholarship (your scholarship, I might add) here in the good ole USA. Fear tells you to slow down because you might get hurt. Fear whispers in your ear, "Are you *sure* this is the right training program? I heard so-and-so is doing so-and-so." Blah, blah, blah.

It's all about fear. If you kill fear, you win. If you kill fear, you have your best year ever. If you kill fear, you train like a madman. If you kill fear, you go to college for free. If you kill fear, you stand on the podium, you get paid, and you have strangers walk up to you and call you by name. When fear dies, you begin to live.

Understanding Fear

In order to understand fear and how it affects our lives, we first must understand where fear comes from—its birthplace.

Most people who really struggle with fear or anxiety, believe that external forces create fear. This external entity could be another person, a past event, or even a possible event in the future.

This simply isn't the case. Instead, fear is created by the person who is experiencing it.

Imagine this scenario:

A toddler is put to bed by his mother, and half an hour passes. The child begins to call for his mother, but she has learned to ignore this behavior, for it will soon pass. Ten minutes later the child is now crying, but it has turned into a distraught cry. The mother goes into the room and finds her child overwhelmed by fear and trembling.

"What's wrong, Honey?" she asks as she embraces her child.

The child explains that there is a monster in the closet. The mother walks to the closet, opens the doors, and proves that there is no monster.

We can all agree that this is a common childhood experience. But, as adults, what can we learn from this?

First, we need to think about where the monster *is*. We know it's nowhere in the room, but then where did the monster come from? The answer is the child's mind.

Second, we need to think about who created the monster. Again, the answer is the child.

But what does this have to do with us? Everything.

Even as babies, we created fictional characters and situations that caused fear. And this is exactly how fear manifests itself throughout our lives. Every fearful or anxious thought we have ever had or will ever have is created by *us*.

So how do we stop this from happening?

KEY TAKEAWAY

Fear is keeping you from reaching your potential.
Conquering fear should be your primary goal in life.

Conquering Fear by Focusing on the Goal

Success over a long period of time is primarily about being singularly focused on one thing—one goal. You have to sell out—that is, make a total mental and physical sacrifice—and fear is the biggest thing keeping you from doing just that.

Selling out is the "Die Trying" approach to life. The willingness to risk it all, to fail big, to be left with nothing when it's over—that is the mindset that we need. Several years ago I was in Bentonville, Arkansas, and I visited the Walmart museum. Sam Walton started Walmart with a small five-and-dime store located on the city square. They had Mr. Walton's old truck and several other small objects that belonged to him on display. One of those objects was his old key chain, which showed the phrase "Go for It."

I thought about writing this book for several years, but I never did it. I had lots of great excuses, and I used every one of them. Then I noticed I was being followed—stalked by this idea of writing—and it made me really uncomfortable. Every time I would begin to have a peaceful moment, I would think about how I was playing scared, running away from taking the risk of saying what I really thought and putting it out there to be judged.

But the truth is, taking risks and challenging yourself leads to opportunity. Conversely, avoiding risk leads to repetition and mediocrity. Taking a risk and putting it all out there is the best way to achieve something you have not yet accomplished.

The worst advice you can give someone who is trying to be successful is to *be careful*. It decreases creativity and risk taking, and it deters performance.

KEY TAKEAWAY

"Be careful" is the worst advice you can give
someone who is trying to do something great.

Your Calling

In comes the concept of being *chosen* rather than making a choice. I like to think of this as being "called." Difficult situations often involve people who are called to be in that place at that time.

Take Aron Ralston. Maybe you remember him. He became famous for cutting his arm off rather than dying in a canyon in Utah. When asked in an interview if making the decision to cut off his arm was the most difficult decision of his life, he replied no. Ralston said the most difficult decision he ever made was the decision to quit his lucrative job at Intel and move to Colorado so he could live as an outdoorsman. He knew that family and friends would be critical of his choice to live his dream, versus live the life that was expected of him. After deciding to pursue his passion at all costs, the decisions that followed were not so difficult. Maybe he was called.

The more ego you have, the more fear you have. Ego makes you self-aware and self-conscious, and it makes you focus on yourself. Ego makes you wonder and care about what others think about you. The less afraid you become, the less you think about yourself, and that allows you to instead think about *what you want*.

What do *you* want? What do you really want? If you could have it any way you please, what would you pick? St. Augustine once said, *Dilige et quod vis fac*: "If you are loving and diligent, you can do whatever you like."

Whatever you like. If you are afraid and undisciplined, which most of us are, you can't do whatever you like because you can't sustain the focus, intention, and energy needed to pull it off.

Do you have something in your life you want badly enough that you are willing to sacrifice everything else in order to achieve it? Keep in mind that if you make this sacrifice, the world will kick your ass. You will be told to "be realistic" or to "think about it" or to "be rational," right? That's the lie that's killing you right now. Greatness is not about being rational and realistic. It's about irrational and crazy thinking.

Chances are that almost everyone you know has given up on themselves and their dreams. So why would they encourage *your* dreams? If you succeed, you will make them more uncomfortable. Average encourages average; mediocre prefers mediocre. In the middle of a competition, there will come a time where you will have the choice to go or not go. I am saying you should *go*.

For most of us, greatness is a threat. Because we haven't achieved it, it's a reminder of what we could be but haven't yet become. Greatness is a lonely, dark road in the middle of nowhere. You will run on it all day and all night, and you'll never see another soul. Every now and then, someone will drive by and say, "Hey, what are you doing way the hell out here? You need to get back into town! You can get hurt out here all by yourself! Jump in and I'll give you a ride."

But you have to risk getting lost because chasing a dream— really chasing it—will lead you to places you never thought were out there. Places no one else would ever care (or dare) to go if they knew about them ahead of time.

If you are like most of us, you never want to venture far enough away from home to risk getting lost.

I have a friend, Tyler Winton, who bought an old Harley-Davidson motorcycle from me, and he drove it all over the country one summer. On a long drive from Texas to Georgia, he pulled off the road and went into a service station to get some gas and splash some water on his face.

He asked the woman at the counter, "What town is this?"

She replied, "Honey, are you lost? Where are you trying to get to?"

"No, ma'am, I'm not lost."

"Well, Honey, if you don't know what town you're in, you're lost."

She missed the point. Tyler knew exactly where he was—in the middle of nowhere on a hero's journey, at some no-name exit off I-20 in Alabama. It doesn't matter where you are, only that you're on your way.

You have to be willing to get lost and wander into uncharted territory. Playing scared keeps you close to the porch, and no one ever got lost or broke a world record in their own backyard. Fear keeps you from wandering around and following an unknown path. Greatness is about taking those paths, every day. You have to be willing to go and figure it out. Average will find you, but you have to go out and hunt for greatness.

In *The Hero with a Thousand Faces*, Joseph Campbell describes the hero's journey this way: Most of us look for a path when we enter a forest. But the hero enters the forest in its deepest and darkest place, where no one has ever entered before. And because he chooses this route, the hero has a very different experience. He faces his demons and the monster that lives in the forest, but when he leaves the forest, he is transformed and changed forever. So you see, the hero is not afraid to get lost, not afraid of the monsters, of failure, and not afraid of death.

Great athletes are on the hero's journey, and they are willing to risk their lives in order to complete their journey. This willingness to die—to make a total sacrifice—is critical. However, I'm not suggesting that you become suicidal in order to reach your goals. But if you become truly fearless, then you are afraid of nothing, including death. Not fearing death doesn't mean you want to die. In fact, accepting the simple fact that you will die someday and that you don't know when that day is coming will help you live more fully.

Fully Committing

In 2013, I was invited to speak to 175 athletes at the University of Arkansas. I asked them, "How many of you would give up two hours a day to become the best athlete in your sport?" All hands went up. Then I asked, "How many of you would be willing to give up four hours a day to be the best?" Again all hands went up. That makes sense because that is the amount of time most college athletes give to their sport each day.

Then I asked them, "How many of you would be willing to totally commit your life to becoming the best in the world?" A few hands went up. Shauna Estes-Taylor, the women's golf coach and former coach of the number one female golfer in the world, Stacy Lewis, was sitting in the front row. Shauna and Stacy are close friends, and they speak regularly. "Shauna," I asked, "would you say that Stacy has totally committed her life to golf in order to be the best?"

181

"Absolutely," said Shauna. Stacy is not the most talented athlete in the world; she was a good player coming out of high school, but she was not highly recruited. She had scoliosis, and she was unable to play her freshman year at Arkansas. It is her heart and her fearless commitment to being the best that have allowed her to be the best female golfer in the world.

The people who acknowledge that they have a limited amount of time and live with a sense of urgency have the best chances of living to their full potential. A fear of death is the same as a fear of life. Fear is fear, even though it comes in all shapes and sizes and 31 different flavors.

The point I'm trying to make is that fear keeps you from staying committed to your goal for a long period of time. Think about someone who is trying to make an Olympic team or, better yet, win a medal. That is a four-year commitment at least. Keeping focused and passionate for four years is very difficult. Only a small group of people can maintain that level of intensity for that extended period of time.

So how do they do it? Hell if I know. Funny thing is, they don't seem to know either. What they do know is that what they are doing is what they are supposed to be doing. Successful people have a great sense of purpose and expectation for their lives. They are on the path of purpose even though they don't truly know where it will lead.

There are a few people who claim to fully understand success, but don't believe a single one of them. You can't follow someone else's path and get there. There is no checklist for success—no map, no GPS, no guarantee, nothing. You have to cut your own path in the woods; fear is the thing that will keep you from doing it.

Just go.

Fear not.

And get yourself lost in your pursuit of success. In your new freedom, you'll find more than you ever thought possible.

21

•————————————•

Only One Way to Tell

If you're going through Hell, keep going.

—WINSTON CHURCHILL

This past holiday, a dear family friend visited our family as she had done many times before. Only one thing was different this time: she brought her new boyfriend, Ken. During our first interaction, I found Ken to be polite, yet very reserved and quiet. Several days into the visit, I learned that Ken was a longtime member of the Army and had been involved with the Special Forces for some time. The U.S. Special Forces work very closely with other countries' Special Forces and perform joint operations throughout the world. More recently, their focus has been in Iraq and Afghanistan fighting terrorist groups like Al-Qaeda.

I soon learned that Ken was not only a member of the Special Forces but he was also a senior ranking officer who was very involved in the selection process as well. We spoke at great length regarding the military's approach to selection and the specific tests they put candidates through to see if they have the temperament to work in the most stressful of all work environments, war.

Ken made it quite clear that although it was okay for me to know general information about what he did, he could not talk about his work, especially the specifics of the missions he had been on and ones he was scheduled to participate in in the future.

Why We Quit

One day, while Ken and I were speaking, he began describing a selection exercise that has been used over time with a great deal of success. The test requires the participants to tread water in a pool about 15 feet deep. There are quite a few soldiers in the water at one time. The instructions are given to the entire group once, and no questions are allowed. Once a whistle is blown, the candidates must swim to the bottom of the pool, touch the floor, and swim back up. There are several underwater observers in scuba gear to confirm that everyone touches the bottom and to ensure that no one drowns.

A wide grin grew on Ken's face as he described how once all the candidates made it to the top of the water, the whistle was blown again, requiring them to go back down after only a quick couple of breaths. Within the first few minutes, candidates would begin to swim to the side of the pool, declaring they either had failed to touch the bottom or could not keep up with the pace of the exercise. They basically disqualified themselves.

Interestingly, there were no instructions given regarding what candidates should do if they failed to touch the bottom or could not go down when the whistle was blown. The candidates just assumed that if they could not complete the task as described, they were automatically out.

Within five minutes, almost all of the candidates would swim to the edge of the pool with looks of frustration and defeat on their face. Then Ken explained, "The only way one could fail the task was to give up. We design it so that no one can complete the task, but we don't care that they can't complete it. We need men who do not give up when faced with an impossible task."

The few that never gave up, never swam over to the side of the pool in defeat, and never thought they had failed, were the ones who would ultimately be chosen to be members of this elite group of men in the Special Forces.

I found the simplicity of that exercise to be genius, and it highlighted something I had witnessed over and over again with the athletes I had worked with. Why do some quit while others continue? Why do some assume they have failed when no one told them they had failed? Why do some refuse to believe they have failed when others insist they are a failure? The message is clear—the only way you can fail is to give up. As long as you are trying, treading water, and gasping for air, you are succeeding.

KEY TAKEAWAY

To fight is to win, to quit is to fail.

Turning It On and Off

This was really juicy stuff, and I asked Ken to tell me more about the traits and characteristics they sought.

"One of the things we look for is a person who can turn it on and turn it off."

It was unclear what he meant, so I asked a question or two about his statement.

"Stan, a lot of men go into the Army because they want to prove that they are tough and not afraid. They want to kick some ass and then go home and tell their friends and family about all the dangerous things they did. We don't want those guys. We look for guys who don't feel like they need to prove their manhood by taking another life. The guys we choose are not overly proud of what they do or how well they do it. They don't get tattoos or walk around with T-shirts that say what they do. That's what I mean by 'turn it off.' When they are not on an operation, they don't think about it, and they don't want to talk about it."

Their jobs don't define them, and they don't need their job to validate them either. At this point, our family friend who was dating Ken chimed in. "Stan, I have been around some of the guys he works with, and you would never know what they do for a living. They are some of the sweetest, most sincere men I have ever met."

I quickly shared how this is also true with great athletes and great leaders as well. When they are at work, it is the most important thing in the world, but when they leave, they don't think about it very much either. The ability to turn it on and turn it off, as Ken defined it, is what allows one to perform at the highest of levels. Turning it off allows people who have achieved at the highest levels to recover and prepare for the next mission and enjoy their time away from their job.

The people who are stressed and unable to recover are the ones who think about their work or sport all the time. They worry, and, in so doing, they deplete their energies and harm their performance. In other words, those who turn it off have the ability to let whatever they are doing in that moment be the most important thing in their life. This is the essence of focus or concentration. Only one thing matters at a time, and that one thing is the most important thing in the world.

Everyone's a Leader

Ken told one last story of a favorite soldier who was on his team. He was a sniper and was a warm and well-respected member of the Army.

I asked Ken what makes a person a great sniper. He answered quickly, "You only take the shot if you are 100 percent sure you can make it. If you're only 99 percent sure, you wait until you get a better shot." Ken described how lesser marksmen allow themselves to feel rushed and pressured into taking a shot. Not the great ones. They will wait all day for the right second because they realize they have to get it right the first time. There are no second chances in that line of work.

One day, while Ken was on a mission with this sniper and four other men, they suddenly found themselves surrounded by the enemy on all sides. There was no way out at the time, and they began to acknowledge that this mission was probably not going to end well. While some of the men began to realize that they may be living their last day, the sniper was thinking differently and said to the group, "They might kill me, but they damn sure are not going to get my chocolate."

He knew that when the enemy killed one of them, they would go through their possessions and take everything they could use. The enemy especially loved chocolate, and the men all had chocolate bars in their food rations that day. The sniper told all the other soldiers to get out the chocolate they had in their packs and eat it. The team followed his advice, and they all began eating the chocolate.

The mood of the team immediately improved. They gained physical energy from the calories and laughed about not letting the enemy eat their chocolate. It was then that they crafted a plan for escaping the enemy and making it out safely without any casualties.

This taught them an invaluable lesson: no matter how desperate your situation may be, there is always something you can do. You are never a victim, and you are never without a choice. The more difficult the situation, the more challenging it is to recognize what options or choices you have. But remember, you always have a choice.

After the story, I asked Ken why the sniper had asserted himself as the leader when Ken was actually the highest-ranking officer in the group. Ken easily explained why. He said, "Oh, that doesn't matter to us. Rank doesn't carry the weight one might think it does on Special

Forces teams. In fact, it's expected that you will disagree with a superior officer if you think his idea is not the best one. That's how we stay alive; we take the best idea no matter whom it comes from."

Ken went on to say that this was not the case in the regular Army. Rank and power are very much adhered to, and soldiers learn early on that they must follow orders. As a general rule, the senior officers have the most experience and are usually correct in the commands they give their troops.

In Special Forces, the rules change. They know that everyone on a Special Forces team is there for a reason. Every person has a specific expertise that the others depend on. Therefore, depending on the issue or situation, the leader or expert changes within the group. Every member is expected to lead and follow and to know when it's their time to lead or follow. Challenging each other is critical to success and survival.

I see the same thing on championship teams. The hero changes from day to day. In fact, the team creates an expectation that everyone will be the hero at some point during the season. Sometimes, an athlete who is not a regular player on a team will step up in a game and make a play that determines the outcome of the game. Coaches of championship teams will frequently allow assistant coaches or even support personnel to play a leading role on the team. These teams talk about how the hero will change throughout the year, and it's important to be ready because you never know when it will be your time to lead the team to victory.

Two years ago, I was watching the University of Georgia swim team practice. They are one of the few programs in which the men and women train together in the pool at the same time. As he does at the end of each practice, Head Coach Jack Baurle (winner of six NCAA championships) picked one of the swimmers to swim a 50-meter time trial. Each time this happens, the swimmer's teammates line the lane to watch.

Jack told everyone that if the swimmer beat a certain time, practice would be over; otherwise, they would swim one more set. This particular practice, the swimmer swam a great time, and the team's practice ended on a high note.

Afterward, I asked Jack why he picked this particular swimmer. Jack explained that this swimmer had a great practice and looked really strong that particular day. I was surprised by his response because most coaches use the exact opposite method. Many coaches would pick an athlete who had not worked hard, and they would use the time trial as a form of punishment or reprimand. Jack had a completely different view on competition though. He saw competing as a privilege and a way for an athlete to represent his or her team and school. Using competition as an honor instead of a punishment makes team members work hard to earn the right to compete.

●————————●

Being with Ken and discussing the topics that we both loved was wonderful. I learned a lot from him, and he confirmed some beliefs I had about performance that I had developed watching athletes and businesspeople.

When it was time for Ken to leave our home, he stuck out his hand, and I said I wanted to give him a hug. He had no problem with that; in fact, he gave me a kiss on the cheek as well. It had been a long time since another man had given me a kiss. Perhaps those who are closest to death are also able to live more passionately and freely.

KEY TAKEAWAY

There are an infinite number of ways to become successful, but there is only one way to become a failure—quit.

Epilogue

To laugh often and much;
to win the respect of intelligent people and the affection of children;
to earn the appreciation of honest critics and
endure the betrayal of false friends;
to appreciate beauty;
to find the best in others;
to leave the world a bit better, whether by a healthy child,
a garden patch or a redeemed social condition;
to know even one life has breathed easier because you have lived.
This is to have succeeded.

—RALPH WALDO EMERSON

I used to believe that I was in control of my life. Now, I believe there is the illusion of control, which is not the same thing as actually being in control. Once our eyes open to this reality, we then get in touch with the better part of ourselves—our soul, the nonphysical self.

With this shift in thinking, we realize that we are motivated not to make more money, win a championship, or win the affection of others.

Instead, we are compelled to be who we are, and we do that by conquering our old selves. By making this change, we can really begin to take flight. We realize we are imprisoned in a world that is no longer acceptable. We can see the other side, and we believe that risking everything, even our lives, is the only thing to do.

These are the times when we have no choice or option. In these times, we do not have the luxury of a decision. It is a *have to*. For me, writing this book became a have to. Whether I wanted to or not, this book was going to be written.

At first, I tried to escape the responsibility, but just like a ghost, it haunted me until I could no longer avoid it. My unconscious mind would wake me up at 2:30, 3:15, or 4:20. I had two choices: lay in bed awake or get up and write. Until then, I never believed in possession, but, sure enough, it happened to me. Some spirit had entered my soul, and I became a possessed man.

After a few days, I quit fighting, and I agreed to just go with it, because if you can't beat 'em, join 'em. Soon, all I had to do was turn on my laptop and just sit there attentively as the words appeared in my head and my fingers magically typed out the thoughts the spirit was speaking to me.

This must be what the artists call a *muse*. In generations before our time, the word *genius* was not used to describe a person but, rather, something that had entered into a person. The genius was not us but some sort of spirit that came from a higher place and temporarily took up residence in one of us. That's what was happening to me. As crazy as it sounds, I didn't write this book, but somehow I will get either the credit or blame for it.

I believe this is one of those experiences that we think is supposed to happen to someone else, someone special. So how could this happen to me? It's simple. It was my time.

And, rest assured your time is coming.

You will not get to pick your time—it will pick you—but your time will definitely come. If you try to hide from it as I did, it will haunt you, wake you up in the middle of the night, and harass you until you finally say, "Okay, I'll do it."

I'm not sure what you will be picked to do. But sooner or later it will be your turn . . . you will be called. And *please, please, please, do not try to avoid it . . . you cannot avoid the call.* We think that those who have achieved greatness did so by their own hard work and dedication. That may be true, but it is not the whole story. They were picked, and they decided to play along with whatever it is out there that does the picking. The people whom I have described in this book all got such a call.

• ———— •

After writing this book, I began to have serious doubts about the quality and potential benefit the book would produce. You can call it a "crisis of confidence." Scotty, one of my editors, regularly told me that the book was coming along well and that it was going to be good. Finally, I got mad at her, and I said, "Quit being nice to me and telling me how good the book is. I need you to be objective." In her own defense, she reminded me that in addition to *writing* a number of articles and books, she had also *read* several thousand, so she had the wisdom and experience to know what is and what isn't a good book. I had to agree with her because she had a pretty objective statement. So, I got up, dusted myself off, and kept going.

After we had finished a first round of edits, we decided that we should send the book out to about five people whom I respect and who could give us some feedback. One of the people I chose to send the draft to was Alicia Shay. I had met Alicia serendipitously in Flagstaff, Arizona, a couple of months earlier. Alicia had run track and cross-country at Stanford University. During her time at Stanford, she had won two NCAA cross-country championships. She also held the NCAA record for the 10,000-meter run. She and her husband, Ryan, had moved to Flagstaff to continue training. Unfortunately, the couple had made national news when Ryan, a very accomplished distance runner, died while competing in the 2008 Olympic marathon trials in New York City. During mile 4 of the race, Ryan collapsed from a cardiac disorder and never regained consciousness. When Alicia arrived at the hospital, she quickly realized that her husband had not fallen and injured his head as she had been told, but that he had died from cardiac failure.

When I met her, it was more than four years later. I had just given a talk to a group of adult runners, and two elite women runners were in the audience. One of the women was Alvina Begay, whom I knew and had worked with in the past. The other was Alicia, but we did not know each other at the time. Alvina was giving me a ride back to my hotel, so I waited for her to finish talking with Alicia. We were introduced, and Alicia asked if she could contact me in the future. She liked my talk, and she had a few things she wanted to speak with me about. I said sure, and when I offered to give her my number, she told me she had already gotten it from Alvina.

When we got in the car, Alvina said, "Do you know who that was?"

When I replied that I didn't, Alvina began to tell me Alicia's story. Soon, I realized that even though I did not know Alicia, I knew her story. Everyone in America who is a distance runner or works with distance runners knows the story of Ryan Shay and the tragedy of his death. I had just met his widow.

It took less than 30 minutes for Alicia to reach out to me by text and thank me for the talk and say she hoped we could talk sometime. I immediately called her back and told her I was leaving at 10 a.m. the next day, but if she would like, we could meet at 7 a.m. the following morning. We met for two hours, and Alicia told me the story of her life and her desire to get healthy and once again become an elite distant runner.

And here we are now, back to the book. I emailed Alicia and asked if she'd had a chance to look at the manuscript I sent her. Here is her email response:

Yes! This is incredible. I still have 30 pages left because I keep going back and reading pages, paragraphs, and sections over. I'll stop doing that so I can finish quickly! :)

All I can say is WOW! I am so thankful that you put this all down in print. [. . .] Each chapter is so rich and spot on. I'm not just blowing steam. I call things pretty straight and honest.

By the way, I think that I mentioned last time we spoke that the residual issues with my hip seem to be clearing up . . . so I want to step on the gas pedal, and I aim to run the NYC [Marathon]. I have eight weeks, and I started workouts last week. It is definitely about half the amount of time I would like to have for my first marathon buildup, but I need to start somewhere, and this could be a really great opportunity! My physio [therapist] is on board, and my coach is coming around to the idea if I can train consistently the next four weeks.

Do you have any thoughts?

I hope your week is going well!
Alicia

P.S. Is your daughter still dropping minute PRs with her compression socks? :)

I immediately picked up the phone and called Alicia. Normally, I don't get an answer when I call her because of her poor reception, but this time, she answered on the first try. I thanked her for reading the book, and again I asked if she thought I should move forward with trying to get published.

"You have to publish this book, Stan. You have to." Immediately, tears started to flow down my face. I had made a promise to myself that if one person benefited from the book, it would have been worth it. I was getting that confirmation now. It had been worth all that I went through. I succeeded. The book did what I hoped it would do . . . help one person. And of all the athletes in the world that I would want to help, Alicia Shay would be my first choice.

After getting the validation I needed, we began to talk about Alicia's goal of running the New York City Marathon. Keep in mind that this is the site where her husband had died five years earlier. The last time she ran in New York City was when she ran through the streets of the crowded city in her street clothes to the hospital after being told Ryan had fallen during the marathon trials. The last time she ran in New York City, she was thinking about her husband and hoping to find him just a little bruised and bloody. This time it would be Alicia running the marathon. She would be the one risking everything to pursue her dream. It took five years, but now Alicia was ready to put her life on the line. It had all come full circle; it was time for closure.

Just as I had needed her confirmation and encouragement for my book, Alicia was asking for my opinion regarding her plan to run the marathon. We talked about what she thought she could run, how she would approach the race, how she would measure success, and what she hoped to accomplish by running the marathon. It was clear to me that she was ready. "Alicia, I am going to give you the same advice you gave me about the book."

"What's that?" she asked.

"Do you remember what you told me when I asked you if you thought I should publish the book?"

"That you have to?"

"Yes, you said I have to publish the book. And you have to run this marathon. You have to."

Sometimes life gives you choices . . . other times you just have to.

In a world full of people, there's so few who can fly. I thank God for the few who dare to fly.

> *These then are my last words to you.*
> *Be not afraid of life.*
> *Believe that life is worth living and*
> *your belief will help create the fact.*

—WILLIAM JAMES

Index

About the Author

Dr. Stan Beecham is a sport psychologist and leadership consultant based in Roswell, Georgia. Legendary coach Vince Dooley gave Beecham his start as an undergraduate student at the University of Georgia (UGA), allowing him to work with Kevin Butler, the great college athlete and professional kicker for the Chicago Bears.

Coach Dooley later hired Dr. Beecham to start the Sport Psychology Program for the Athletic Department, and Dr. Beecham was instrumental in helping UGA win numerous individual and team championships during his tenure.

Today his work with collegiate, Olympic, and professional athletes from many sports has afforded him an insight into the minds of great competitors that only a few have had the good fortune to gain.

Dr. Beecham has taken his wisdom into the business world as he develops and conducts leadership programs for corporate clients.

A world-class speaker and presenter, Dr. Beecham shares his vast knowledge and experience in this incredible work.

Contact the author at
www.DrStanBeecham.com